Peter Eckersley

The Flying Cricketer

Rev. Malcolm G. Lorimer

Max Books

© Rev. Malcolm G. Lorimer 2023

First published in the UK in 2023 by Max Books

The right of Rev. Malcolm G. Lorimer to be identified as the Author of this work has been asserted by him in accordance with the Copyright, Designs and Patents Act 1988

All rights reserved. Apart from any use permitted under UK copyright law no part of this publication may be reproduced, stored in a retrieval system, or transmitted, in any form or by any means, without the prior written permission of the publisher, nor be otherwise circulated in any form of binding or cover other than that in which it is published and without a similar condition being imposed on the subsequent purchaser

A CIP catalogue record for this title is available from the British Library

ISBN: 978-1-9196389-2-8

Typeset and Design by Andrew Searle

Printed and bound in India

MAX BOOKS
2 Newbold Way
Nantwich
CW5 7AX
Email: maxcricket@btinternet.com
www.max-books.co.uk

Contents

Foreword *by Stephen Chalke* — 4

Introduction — 7

1. Charisma — 9

2. Loyalty — 23

3. Leadership — 39

4. Exotic climes — 61

5. Courage — 81

6. Sacrifice — 91

7. Tribute to a gallant man — 99

8. Not forgotten — 109

Appendices — 113

Acknowledgements — 143

Foreword

by Stephen Chalke

WHAT A FASCINATING character is Peter Eckersley! He was clearly blessed with a joy of life, boundless energy and great self-confidence. He captained Lancashire at cricket for seven summers, winning two county championships; he became a skilled pilot, with his own plane, in those early years of air flight in the 1920s; and he was elected to parliament – all before his 32nd birthday.

A natural adventurer, eager to take on fresh challenges, he undertook several private cricket tours around the world, he broke precedent by flying the whole Lancashire eleven to avoid a long train journey. Then, when his political career was fast developing and war was declared, he defied those who said he was too old and joined the Fleet Air Arm, dying when his plane crashed on a training exercise. He was just 36 years old.

How fortunate we are that his grandson William, chancing on a box of memorabilia in his father's garage, should think to bring them to Old Trafford – and that Malcolm Lorimer, that most dedicated of archivists, should see immediately the specialness of what the scrapbooks and photographs revealed. For Peter Eckersley's story is indeed special, unique even.

What can it have been like for a young man of 24, as Peter Eckersley was in 1929, to take on the captaincy of the Lancashire county side? Under Colonel Leonard Green, 14 years his senior, they had won three championships in a row. They were a well-established group, a hard bunch of northern professionals, and they were now in the hands of a youngster who batted with dash but no great consistency, who had not even made the eleven at Cambridge University.

The words of the Yorkshire batsman Maurice Leyland, talking of his own county's captains in those years, come to mind: "We won a few championships with the handicap of one."

Yet Peter Eckersley, it seems, was no handicap to them. His love of life and his spirit of adventure were infectious, and he was easy and relaxed in his dealings with his team. When it mattered, when a championship title was in prospect, he knew how to adapt his personality to the hard-grafting culture of the professionals. It may have upset that incorrigible romantic Neville Cardus, but he was happy for his men to settle for first-innings points in a dull draw rather than risk all in an unpredictable dash for victory.

His seven years at the helm make him Lancashire's longest-serving captain since the First World War, and his team's two outright championships are more than the county has won in almost 80 years since. The first, in his second year in charge, drew on the strength of the team he inherited from Leonard Green. The second, four years later, was the greater achievement, drawing on a new generation that he had nurtured and moulded into winners.

How odd that his story should have been so neglected in the years since his death in 1940! We owe a gratitude to Malcolm Lorimer, and to grandson William, for restoring his reputation with this delightful book.

Introduction

IT WAS IN August 2021 when a young man walked into the Lancashire reception carrying a very large cardboard box. Lancashire were playing Warwickshire and he asked to see me in the 1864 Suite where he opened his box of treasures.

His name was William Eckersley and he was the grandson of one of Lancashire's most charismatic players and captains, but one who it seemed everyone had forgotten: Peter Eckersley. William told a remarkable story of his father and his relationship with his grandfather.

PETER THORP ECKERSLEY was born in Newton-le-Willows and there were pictures of the family house as well as the church where there is a stained glass window commemorating his achievements.

The box, which had lain forgotten in his father's flat for many years, contained scrapbooks of Peter's cricketing career including albums of some of the cricket tours he went on to India, Jamaica and Argentina.

His political life was well documented from when he unsuccessfully contested Leigh for the Conservatives until he was elected in 1935 for the Manchester Exchange seat. As a consequence he resigned the Lancashire captaincy to go into politics. In February 1940 he was appointed Parliamentary Private Secretary to Major Lloyd George, who was then Secretary to the Board of Trade.

There were photos aplenty with the Lancashire teams of the 1930s and some good photos of his fellow teammates, and one especially when he piloted the Lancashire team from Wales to Southampton in 1934. He made history as it was the first time a county team had flown to a cricket match (some of the team look very nervous).

Known as the 'cricketing-airman', he obtained his Flying Certificate in 1928 with the Lancashire Flying Club, and he joined the Royal Aeronautical Club in 1929. With a fascination for all things flying, which figured in his untimely death, he often flew his aeroplane to matches and he made cricketing history when he chartered a plane in his first full season to fly his team from Swansea to Southampton.

In a team of hardened Lancashire professionals, he had the unenviable job of following Col. Leonard Green, who had captained Lancashire to three County Championships in a row and Peter was then only 24. He astounded his critics by winning the County Championship in 1930 and also in 1934. It would be another 77 years before Lancashire lifted the trophy outright again.

There was a beautiful album of family photographs including of a holiday in Switzerland with Peter skiing and tobogganing with the fantastic photo of Peter and his wife Audrey standing on the running board of his 1928 Bentley, which is still going strong 85 years later.

The scrapbooks detail Peter's cricketing career spanning the years 1923-1936 when he scored 5,629 runs with an average of 19.54, including one century against Gloucestershire at Bristol. He was a very good close-in fielder, holding 141 catches.

His tragic death while piloting a training aircraft in the Royal Naval Volunteer Reserve at Eastleigh is also forgotten, with no memorial. There was a 'political' dispute at the time between the services which seemed to ignore the efforts of the RNVR.

Lancashire have a memorial for the cricketers lost in the First World War but we realised we had forgotten one of the most successful, courageous and charismatic captains to have led the team. We needed to put that right and have a memorial for the Second World War. There is a memorial to Peter at Bowdon CC and also a stained glass window in Astley.

In September 2022, during the County Championship match against Yorkshire, a fitting memorial to the bravery of Lt. Peter Thorp Eckersley, one of Lancashire's most charismatic and courageous players, was unveiled. It was very appropriate that Peter's grandson William unveiled the plaque, and also present were family members of naval gunner Sidney Snow, who was also killed in the air crash.

Rev. Malcolm Lorimer
Lancashire Heritage Team

1.

Charisma

"Charisma is the intangible that makes people want to follow you, to be around you, to be influenced by you."
Roger Dawson

A young Peter with parents William and Eva.

I WONDER IF you are born with charisma or it is something that develops over the years? It certainly cannot be taught or bought. Peter Thorp Eckersley was described by those who knew him as someone imbued with that most elusive of qualities. Whether it was on the cricket field, in the House of Commons, flying light aircraft or pursuing some of the more dangerous sports, this is what people admired about the man.

Peter was born on the 2nd July 1904 at Lowton, Newton-le-Willows, Lancashire. He was the only son of Eva Mary Eckersley (JP) of Tyldesley and William Eckersley (CBE and JP), master cotton spinner. His grandfather was Charles Eckersley, of Tyldesley, head of Messrs. Caleb Wright and Co, a large cotton milling company.

Perhaps it was from his parents he inherited the interest in politics and public service, something that would stay with him the rest of his short life and also mean that cricket would be put aside to pursue a career in politics and public service. His father was Chairman for some years of the North Western Area Liberal Unionist Party and his mother Eva was for many years Chair of the North Western Area Unionists. She was also a Justice of the Peace.

The surname Eckersley is an old Lancashire name with Anglo-Saxon origins and is the name for a 'lost village' or hamlet or woodland clearing. The family can trace its roots back to the Middle Ages *(see footnote 1)*.

The family home where Peter grew up was Lime House, Lowton, which was built by Peter's father in 1903 on the site of an older house with about 20 acres and was part of the Bridgewater estate *(see footnote 2)*. Peter was born at the house on the 2nd July 1904. The house was boarded by a hall wall the whole length of the property on Newton Road and Heath Lane down to the main gate. A local resident remembers:

> *My earliest memories were of the high wall running the whole length of the property on Newton Road and down Heath Lane to the main gate. The large entrance drive onto Newton Road was part of the alterations made by the Golborne Urban District council in 1935.*
>
> *As young boys we would climb the wall to peep over on to the lawns hoping to see the famous amateur cricketers, many of whom were entertained during*

their matches with Lancashire. Rumours would go around that Ranji or A.P.F. Chapman were staying the weekend, but I must confess that I never saw any of them. Delegations of boys went occasionally to ask for cast-off bats and were not often disappointed. Many of the bats found their way on to Highfield Moss to be used by all the locals, In the 1920s it is doubtful if we would have had a cricket bat to play with but for the generosity of Mr. P.T. Eckersley.

Peter went to Stanmore Park School in 1913, which was a preparatory school for Public Schools. In the late 1880s Herbert Kemball Cook's preparatory school was transferred from Brighton to Stanmore Park, which was described as 'a large mansion with extensive grounds off Uxbridge Road, Stanmore'. The headmaster from 1901 to 1929 was former Lancashire and England cricketer Rev. Vernon Royle.

Royle played in only the third ever Test Match at Melbourne in 1879, making him Lancashire's first Test Cricketer. He had a pleasant batting style with a powerful straight drive and a sound defence. But it would be for his fielding he would be remembered, as a cover fielder he had no equal.

Rev. Vernon Royle

He was a teacher at Elstree School and was ordained as a clergyman in the Church of England before taking up the position of headmaster to Stanmore Preparatory School. In the Lancashire Library archive we have around forty sermons which were delivered by Vernon Royle while he was Headmaster at the school. Sadly, we can find no mention of cricket, but that is not say that he didn't inspire his young protégés and in 1929 as President of Lancashire it would surely have been a very proud moment for him to see Peter Eckersley play for Lancashire as captain. Sadly, Vernon Royle died in May 1929, the year before Peter led Lancashire to the County Championship.

At the age of fourteen Peter transferred to Rugby School and he spent from 1918 to 1922 there. The school newspaper, *The Meteor*, records over the next few years Peter playing for the school cricket team and also house matches. Reports mention that he distinguished himself in the team and for some matches he also kept wicket. In 1921 with scores of 72 and 84, both not out, he was congratulated on making the Rugby XI and is pictured in the school team. He played at Lord's in the annual match against Marlborough in 1922 when Rugby lost. The school gave Peter a good grounding in the game of cricket.

He also played other sports, distinguishing himself at Racquets and Rugby Union as well as Football and Hockey. He continued to play Racquets after leaving the school and there is mention of him coming back to the school with H.E. Stanford on a tour to play at the school in the late 1920s. He also attended the school Speech Day, scoring 86 in a cricket match against the school in 1924.

In 1922 at the age of 19 Peter went to Trinity College, Cambridge for two years. He took examinations for the first part of a law degree in March 1923, but does not appear to have sat any other examinations or to have taken a degree. His personal tutor at Trinity was Frederick James Dykes, who was an engineer, but tutors didn't always specialise in the same subject as their students. In his first year Peter lived at 36 Sidney Street and in Whewell's Court in his second. In looking at the index of clubs and societies there is no record of him and, surprisingly, he didn't play cricket for the college.

It appeared that when leaving Cambridge Peter had many opportunities before him. He could have followed his father into business and as his father was in the final years of his life there would have been pressure to follow in his footsteps. But you couldn't see Peter being content sitting behind a desk; his spirit was for adventure, dangerous sports and flying light aircraft.

The lure of politics was strong and over the next few years Peter would make two serious attempts at being elected M.P. for local constituencies. Then there was cricket and it seems that the influence of friends like the Higsons were pivotal in persuading him to make a career in cricket, at least while he was in his twenties.

Back home

Lime House came into the possession of Peter on the death of his father in 1925. There was an old coachman still working there, though the horses he had been so proud of had long been replaced by the limousine. Mr Coe, the head gardener, still kept the grounds in immaculate condition.

Aerial photograph of Peter Eckersley's birthplace, Lime House in Lowton, taken from his Avian GAABX (inset) in the Summer of 1932.

In 1935 it was sold to Golborne Urban District Council for offices. Later Wigan Metro became the owners before they disposed of the property to a Catholic Charity who adapted the buildings to make a very pleasing home for the elderly.

Another local resident Alec Hughes tells of his childhood memories of Mr Eckersley's plane landing on the fields behind his home. Several times in the 1920s he landed his bi-plane on 'Mr. Rigby's' field at Locking Stoops Farm. His future wife Audrey was also keen on flying and a member of The

Lancashire Aero Club where Peter was Chairman. From 1937 to 1939 he owned an Avro Avian G-AABX and often flew to cricket matches.

The family were keen Unitarians, which was very strong in the North West of England, and was also very influential in many of its members being active in politics. The family chapel was Chowbent Unitarian Chapel, Atherton where the Eckersley's had a family pew and later on in June 1930 Peter and Audrey would be married in the chapel.

Chowbent Chapel

One of the members, Mrs Stroud, remembers:

Peter with his young wife and family coming to the services, I will always remember Peter in his smart military uniform with its pilot's wings.

In the chapel there still is the family pew and stained-glass window with the inscription:

Pro Patria
Lt(a) Peter Thorp Eckersley
R.N.V.R. J.P. M.P.
A trustee of Chowbent Chapel
Born 2nd July 1904
Killed flying on active service
13th August 1940.
Devoted remembrance from
His wife, mother and sister

Mr & Mrs Eckersley

Engaged to childhood sweetheart

Peter was about ten years old when he met his childhood sweetheart who was later to become his wife, Audrey Hyde Johnson. He said that *"He had a great admiration for her from the beginning and from childhood companions we became sweethearts and lovers."* The romance developed out of a long friendship between the mothers of the couple.

Audrey was a keen cricket enthusiast, but she was more deeply involved in aviation and they did a lot of flying together. Peter was Chairman of the Lancashire Aero Club and owned a plane which he kept at Chat Moss Aerodrome. Audrey also flew and was at the time of their marriage in 1930 qualifying as a pilot in her own right. She was a great admirer of her namesake Amy Johnson. Peter had a pilot's licence for over two years and was awaiting the time when his fiancée was able to take charge of an aeroplane. *"The two lovers will spend much of their time together in the clouds"* reported a local newspaper.

At the announcement of their engagement in 1929 (Peter was 25) Audrey was living in London and was staying at Lime House with Peter's mother. They received congratulatory telegrams from all parts of the country.

During their time together they played golf and were both accomplished players but not seriously interested in the game except from the point of view of recreation.

On the 20th June 1930 Peter married Audrey Estelle Ljufling Hyde-Johnson of Ashley, Cheshire. One of the iconic photos of Peter and Audrey is taken on holiday in France with the pair standing beside their 1927 Bentley. Peter purchased the car from Kenneth Dobson, a Royal Navy Officer from Derbyshire who played cricket for both Derbyshire and Warwickshire and was a goalkeeper for Derby County Football Club.

Peter and Audrey enjoyed the Bentley, often taking it abroad on holidays to foreign climes. The family photo albums detail many of the holidays.

    1930 - driving to Algiers and Sahara via Marseille
    1931 - skiing holiday in Diablerets
    1932 - Las Palmas via *S.S. Highland Princess*
    1932 - Blackpool

1932 - driving to Juan Les Pins, South of France, Switzerland (Diablerets) and Ypres

1933 - driving through Spain and France via San Sebastián, Burgos, Toledo, St. Jean de Luz, Angouleme

1934 - skiing holiday in Diablerets and Gstaad

1934 - cricket trip and holiday in Portugal, inc Lisbon, Oporto, Vigo via R.M.M.V. Asturias

1934 - Blackpool

1934 - Rhos-On-Sea

Plus various others, inc. Austria and eastern Europe

The iconic photo of Peter and Audrey with their 1927 Bentley.

The albums testify to Peter and Audrey's love of adventurous and often dangerous sports. The winter sports of skiing, tobogganing, bobsleigh and ice skating among the other sports.

Light aircraft flying was not without its dangers in the 1930s. Flying was still in its infancy and accidents often happened. Peter and Audrey were mainly flying single engine planes by themselves.

If anyone can be describes as having charisma then Peter Thorp Eckersley was blessed with it because of his likeable personality, leadership qualities and love of adventure and excitement. Shown in the winter holidays and sports on ice, owning the 1928 Bentley and the cricket tours to exotic climes. The thrill of piloting light aircraft and not least the desire to serve his fellow man in wanting to become a Member of Parliament and, of course, the sacrifice he was prepared to make in volunteering to serve in the Naval Air Reserve in the war.

Footnote 1

This interesting surname, with the variant Eccersley, is of Anglo-Saxon origin, and is a locational name from some minor or unrecorded place, perhaps a "lost" village. There are an estimated seven to ten thousand villages and hamlets that have now disappeared from Britain since the 12th Century; the prime cause of these "disappearances" was the enforced "clearing" and dispersal of the former inhabitants to make way for sheep pastures at the height of the wool trade in the 15th Century, and natural causes such as the Black Death of 1348, in which an eighth of the population perished. The original place is believed to have been in the parish of Leigh, near Wigan, in Lancashire, and is so called from the genitive case of the Olde English pre 7th Century personal name "Ecgheard" (from the Germanic given name "Eckhardt", composed of the elements "agi(n)", edge, point, and "hard", hardy, brave, strong), and the Olde English "leah", wood, clearing. Recordings of the surname from English Church Registers include: the christening of Richard Eckersley on February 10th 1576, at Leigh, Lancashire; the marriage of William Eckersley and Ellen Geste on July 25th 1593, in the same place; and the christening of Mary, daughter of George Eckersley, in January 1682, at Badworth, Yorkshire.

The first recorded spelling of the family name is shown to be that of Henry de Eccleseye, which was dated 1301, in the "Early Medieval Records of Yorkshire", during the reign of King Edward 1, known as "The Hammer of the Scots", 1272 - 1307. Surnames became necessary when governments introduced personal taxation. In England this was known as Poll Tax. Throughout the centuries, surnames in every country have continued to "develop" often leading to astonishing variants of the original spelling.

Read more: https://www.surnamedb.com/Surname Eckersley#ixzz7P0q0kNzY

Footnote 2

Here is what a local resident had to say about the house in a local magazine:

Lime House, Lowton was built in 1903 by a wealthy millowner, Mr William Eckersley, on the site of an older property of the same name, though on one or two of the census returns the spelling Lyme House was used. The old house must also have been quite large according to the returns of 1841-81 which show that in each case several servants were kept. During that period the occupants were all Liverpool businessmen; one, a W.H. Livesey, was chief accountant to the Mersey Dock and Harbour Board. The property extending to about 20 acres was part of the Bridgewater Estate and all the tenants seem to have maintained a nursery until Mr Eckersley became the owner. The 1881 census records that Mr.R. Milner resided there with his young wife and his own grown-up family; he was 65 - his wife 36. Although it is not shown in the census, Mr. Milner had a daughter, Mary Ann, who eloped one night with Enoch Sankey, a handsome young farmer from Croft. She escaped through the bedroom using a ladder that had been conveniently left nearby. Mr Sankey became one of the biggest horse dealers in Europe before and during the 1914 war. There are many stories told of his flamboyant character, who was always dressed as a wealthy farmer with bowler hat, expensive waistcoat, breeches and highly polished top boots. The one I heard when I was very young recounts that he liked to gamble, and that one night in a Liverpool hotel he was winning heavily and wanted a reason to get away; he excused himself for a few minutes during which time he telephoned Lime Street Station to book a special train to Kenyon Station for "Lord Croft". He returned to the table for a while before he announced that his special coach awaited him at Lime Street. The disbelieving company followed him to find that Lord Croft had indeed a coach waiting for him.'

In 1887 Mr W.H. Arnott became the owner and occupier. He had the paper mill at Golborne, and still maintained the nursery - in fact a large vinery was shown on the plans at the time of purchase. The Arnott's sold Lime House in 1902 to Mr. Eckersley who was responsible for building the new house in 1903.

I WISH TO MARK, BY THIS PERSONAL MESSAGE, my appreciation of the service you have rendered to your Country in 1939.

In the early days of the War you opened your door to strangers who were in need of shelter, & offered to share your home with them.

I know that to this unselfish task you have sacrificed much of your own comfort, & that it could not have been achieved without the loyal co-operation of all in your household.

By your sympathy you have earned the gratitude of those to whom you have shown hospitality, & by your readiness to serve you have helped the State in a work of great value.

Elizabeth R

P. Eckersley, Esq.

2.

Loyalty

"You stand up for your teammates. Your loyalty is to them. You protect them through good and bad, because they'd do the same for you."

Yogi Berra, catcher, New York Yankees Baseball team

Myles Kenyon

Jack Sharp

Col. Leonard Green

Peter Eckersley

Lionel Lister

Lancashire's five captains between the wars

In the years between the wars five captains, Myles Kenyon, Jack Sharp, Col. Leonard Green, Peter Eckersley and Lionel Lister, led Lancashire with varying degrees of success. Leonard Green and Peter Eckersley merit distinction with five County Championships between them whilst such honours eluded the other three.

To set Peter's success in context it is worth looking at the attributes and styles of the other captains and what kind of team Lancashire were between the wars. Each captain was different with contrasting abilities and personalities, but they all had unflagging zeal for everything connected with Lancashire cricket and an almost fanatical regard for the welfare of the professionals in their charge. The care of the professionals was something which marked Lancashire out from other counties, who seemed to regard their professionals as second-class citizens. The Lancashire captains were rewarded with something missed by other county captains: respect and loyalty.

Myles Kenyon took over as Lancashire captain after the First World War. It was a very big job and he was only a club cricketer with no experience of the first-class game. Added to this he had a pretty tough bunch of players to deal with. It would have been easy for any man in such circumstances to be overwhelmed and eventually finding the tail wagging the dog, as it were. Underneath his seeming inexperience and undoubtedly kindly outlook on life, which could have been mistaken for weakness as far as leadership was concerned, was a will of steel.

The Lancashire players soon realised that there was going to be one boss, and one boss only on the field: Myles Kenyon. It was a tough situation. They did not react kindly to being led by someone whom they regarded as a passenger. But Kenyon gradually overcame their prejudices and it wasn't long before he had them completely under his spell, so much so that they united in their endeavours to disguise his shortcomings, particularly in the field.

If he was fielding at mid-on and a skyer went up Cec Parkin would yell "mine skipper" and dash across from mid-off to take the catch. If he were fielding at mid-off and a similar situation arose the same cry of "mine skipper" would come from Harry Makepeace at cover. The beauty of all this was that Kenyon did not regard it as an impertinent affront; neither did the players look on it as an opportunity to discredit Kenyon in the eyes of the spectators. The feeling was simply that it was all for the benefit of the team. More important was the overall feeling that "if the skipper is good to us, we'll pull our guts out for him," a quality of all the Lancashire sides between the wars. This is how Lancashire's great team spirit between the wars was born. (It is worth noting that when Lancashire tried this again in 1964 with the appointment of an amateur captain, Joe Blackledge, it didn't work.)

This same attitude was carried on by the next captain, Jack Sharp. His problem was different though. He had a wonderful cricket career and had played for England at both cricket and football. An eminently successful businessman, he had built up a flourishing sports outfitting business in Liverpool. As an ex-professional the big question was how would the players react to the taking of orders from a captain who had previously been "one of them". In the event the problem rarely arose. What did cause him some concern was the public reaction to his appointment. There seemed to be a feeling of antipathy, particularly amongst the spectators. They were quick to react to his slightest error and vocal demonstrations of their disapproval were by no means rare.

The professionals stood by him loyally and gave him their fullest support. But he was fighting a losing battle. The showdown was tragic in that it happened on an occasion which was meant to have been Old Trafford's showpiece of the era - Cec Parkin's benefit match in 1925. A military band had been engaged to entertain the crowds before play started and during the intervals, something hitherto unknown in the prosaic north. Parkin was one of the liveliest characters in cricket and undoubtedly a great crowd-puller. The stage was set for an epic three days but a malignant fate decided otherwise.

The start was sensational. Middlesex opening batsman Harry Lee gently pushed Parkin's first delivery to short leg to offer Jack Sharp the simplest of chances. It was described as the sort of catch one would lob to a five-year-old child and expect it to be caught. To everyone's consternation Sharp took his eye off the ball and dropped the catch. There was a stupefied silence for a second or two, then the storm broke. The spectators jeered and hurled taunts at Sharp. They suggested he had missed the catch deliberately so as to make the match last three days. From that moment onwards the spectators made Jack Sharp's life a living hell. Every time he touched the ball, he was the target for jeers and catcalls. At the end of the game, he was a heartbroken man. He wanted to relinquish the captaincy and vowed he would never again play at Old Trafford. The Lancashire committee persuaded him to reconsider his decision and he carried on. But he was never comfortable and it was no surprise when he announced his retirement from the game at the end of the 1925 season.

Perhaps Jack Sharp's biggest mistake was accepting the captaincy in the first instance. No doubt he considered it a great honour, but at 45 he was well past his best in both ability and agility. The Lancashire committee learned a lesson from this. Leonard Green was 36 when he took over and Peter Eckersley and Lionel Lister were only 24 when they assumed responsibility.

Col. Leonard Green was a man of great personal charm, as was to be expected of a soldier who was a strict disciplinarian too. Much to the delight of the Lancashire players he emerged as one who preferred the velvet glove to the rod of iron. He could nevertheless wield the big stick if the occasion demanded. Such was his popularity that such occasions were few and far between. One such occurred during an end of season tour in Scotland. Let all-rounder Len Hopwood recount the story:

> We were due to play an Army XI at Forres. In the Lancashire side was the great fast bowler Ted McDonald whom the Army side had every reason to fear. They decided to spike his guns. He spent the night before the match as their guest in the Officers' mess. During the course of what must have been a riotous party "Mac" gleaned information about Leonard Green's career as a soldier which everyone knew had been an illustrious one.
>
> In a burst of alcoholic candour one of the officers revealed that Green had a certain nickname in Army circles. It was one of those which while on the face of things appearing derisory are affectionately bestowed on persons.
>
> The following morning broke bright and clear. Mac was in the marquee on the ground enjoying a 'hair of a dog' that bit him with his colleagues of

the night before. Leonard Green appeared on the scene with a cheerful "Good Morning, Mac."

"Good morning, Blossom" replied Mac. Green stopped in his tracks. He spoke quietly. "I beg your pardon, Mac?" The greeting was repeated, but this time with a bit less confidence.

There was a deathly hush in the marquee. Players of both sides realised that here was a situation which had developed far beyond the humorous.

All eyes were focused on Green. He soon settled the issue. "Mac, you can either apologise publicly now or get the next train back to Manchester."

Mac's response was awaited with bated breath. It came in two words. "Sorry skipper." And that was that. It was all over. Col. Green never again referred to the incident.

The potential crisis was averted by two great hearted men. One strong enough to insist, and rightly so, on the maintenance of the dignity of his position as captain of Lancashire, the other big enough to realise his mistake and publicly acknowledge it. Len Hopwood, asked about who he thought was the best captain, unhesitatingly plumped for Colonel Leonard Green. *"There have been better cricketers,"* he remarked, *"but as a captain Colonel Green stood alone. He exercised discipline with a minimum of fuss, was a shrewd thinker, and while having a mind of his own was never afraid to turn to his senior professional for advice. Above all, he had the great attribute of getting the best out of his team. In return we would have played our guts out for him."*

Leonard Green had a great capacity for getting the best out of his men. His hat-trick of Championships in 1926-1927-1928 was sufficient evidence of that. It would be these big shoes that 24-year-old Peter Eckersley would be stepping into after Green's retirement. It says much about him that he was not nervous or unduly worried about the task before him. Only a modest player himself, he had the qualities of leadership and charisma which would see him follow the success of Col. Green and bring the best out of the players. When he took over he inherited two great assets, a damn fine side and the benefits of a three-year apprenticeship with Leonard Green. The traditions of the Lancashire team built up since Myles Kenyon were in safe hands.

And that wasn't all. The older members of the team had seen Peter Eckersley grow up and the younger professionals, like Hopwood and Duckworth, had grown up with the skipper. He in turn saw to it that nothing was lacking in his endeavours to promote the welfare of those who were doing so much for him. On one occasion the team were faced with a diabolical journey from Swansea to Southampton. This necessitated hours of weary travel by train and an arrival at Southampton at some ungodly hour. Peter would have none of it. He chartered two small planes - at his own expense - and they landed in Southampton not as a travel-strained, weary bunch but as a team absolutely exhilarated by the distinction of being the first county cricket team to travel by air to a match.

Look at that 1928 side which Peter inherited. The County Championship had been won for the third successive year with 15 wins and not a single defeat. The Lancashire batting in 1928 was the strongest it has ever been with three players, Hallows, Watson and Ernest Tyldesley each scoring over 2,000 runs. The bowling was in the hands of Ted McDonald with 190 wickets and Dick Tyldesley with 104 wickets. George Duckworth was his reliable self behind the wicket and they were a formidable side.

The Heavy Brigade

There was also another side to the Lancashire side of late 20s to early 30s - the notorious 'heavy brigade'. How would the young amateur fresh from Cambridge deal with them? Stories of their escapades, of their practical joking and of their seemingly unquenchable thirsts were legion. The team which won the championship three years in a row and also in 1930 was relatively unchanged with some very strong professionals and full-blooded extrovert characters. Confident in their ability to produce the goods on the field, they had few inhibitions in their free time off it. Dick Tyldesley used to say *"this game's worth it for t'neets."*

They were cricketers who knew their worth, the professionals who more or less formed the regular squad: Makepeace, Hallows, Tyldesley(E), Watson, Tyldesley(R), Parkin, Iddon, Hopwood, Duckworth, McDonald and Sibbles. Only Frank Watson and Frank Sibbles failed to get international honours. Watson got a consolation MCC tour to the West Indies and

Sibbles had to be content with a Test Trial. Many less talented players than these two have worn England caps.

Here are a few of the stories told by Len Hopwood of the great Championship winning sides who completed the hat-trick of wins.

> *They were a rare handful for any captain. But once that captain had earned their respect he was assured of their loyalty and support. In striking contrast, they had little time for the committee room, whom they alleged 'couldn't run a bloody chip shop.' Any committee suggestion that steps might be taken to curtail their off-field enjoyment was scoffed at. 'Let em try it,' they would say.*

The committee did try it. They experimented with a policy of sending a committeeman to accompany the team to away matches, to act as a sort of restraining father figure and to keep an eye open for any untoward incidents. It was doomed to failure form the start. Mr Johnny Fallows, father of the future chairman of Lancashire was the committeeman in charge at Gloucester. Mr Charlie Williams officiated at Southend. Both were men of charm but they were never in with a chance. Neither possessed the low cunning or the ruthlessness necessary to outwit 'The Heavy Brigade', past masters of leg pull and chicanery.

The committeemen returned to Old Trafford with their expenses' sheets loaded with the cost of drinks they had been inveigled into buying for the lads. So skilful in this art were 'The Heavy Brigade' that it was only when the victim came to the final balance of his accounts that he realised how craftily and almost unknowingly he had been taken for a ride. Two matches were enough. The committee dropped the experiment. It was too expensive. Not only that, they found themselves in the ludicrous position of paying for the drinking which they were trying to curtail!

Another time Lancashire were playing at Northampton and they had a curfew to be in bed for 10.30, but at midnight Len Hopwood was awakened by strange nocturnal sounds:

> *A peep through the window revealed a conglomeration of humans struggling up a ladder (borrowed from a nearby brewery) to get into their rooms at the guest house. There they were, Cec Parkin, Dick Tyldesley, and Ted McDonald*

The 1926 county champions – The Heavy Brigade

struggling to get the Evening News reporter Johnny Clegg and themselves through the window. Harry Makepeace, the senior professional, was directing operations from the bottom of the ladder.

The cunning and tricks of the Heavy Brigade could never be doubted and there wasn't a shrewder brain in the game than Harry Makepeace.

He came up with a brilliant stroke in the 1920s. We had to travel from Old Trafford to Eastbourne to play Sussex. Makepeace found out that one of the umpires, Doc Young, was faced with the same long journey.

There was a near riot when our senior professional calmly informed us that he had invited Doc Young to travel with us in our saloon. Young was a great character but a lot too garrulous for most of us. The prospect of having to listen to his chatter for hours on end was enough to drive us up the wall. Protests were waved aside by Makepeace who had also made arrangements for an adequate supply of beer to be available in the saloon.

We were mystified when he began to make a fuss of Young. George Duckworth could stand it no longer. He got Harry on one side and asked. "What the hell is the big idea?"

Mystification turned to hilarity when the plan was unfolded. Young, a former Essex player, was for ever recalling a colossal hit he had made "over the bleedin elms" at Eastbourne. That hit was to be the principal subject of comment the following day. We lost the toss. Within half-an-hour every Lancashire player had fielded in the vicinity of Young's umpiring position, had gazed in the direction of the boundary and had expressed amazement at the length of that hit 'over the bleedin elms'.

Whether the favourable response to ensuing LBW appeals were mere coincidence or the result of Makepeace cunning we will never know.

A friend remarked to Len Hopwood, "*Some of that lot you played with could sup ale.*" "*Yes,*" he replied. "*They could also play cricket too.*"

That was what the disciplinarians found themselves up against. These players could point to their record during this period. From 1919 to 1930 they won the County championship four times, were runners-up twice, third on two other occasions, once fourth and never below fifth place.

But things would change in the 1930s; the great side of the twenties was slowly been broken up with retirements and only the championship in 1934 remained. That it would be another 77 years before Lancashire again won the title outright shows perhaps what a great side this had become under the shrewd captaincy of Col. Green and Peter Eckersley.

When Peter Eckersley retired to go into politics in 1935, Lionel Lister took over as captain at the same age as Eckersley. He had a very different experience though and in the five seasons up to the war could not sustain a challenge for the championship. As a cricketer he was streets ahead of his predecessors - an attacking batsman of rare power and during his early years with Lancashire he promised great things. Playing against Larwood and Voce in 1934, bowling short-pitch 'Bodyline' deliveries, he stood his ground and hooked again and again. More than once he escaped decapitation by a mere hair's breadth, but he refused to be intimidated. This innings was fit to rank amongst one of the great innings for the county.

Unfortunately, his batsmanship never blossomed into the glory everyone had anticipated. Perhaps the responsibilities of captaincy had something to do with the regrettable stunt in the growth of his undoubted talent.

His early promise in the leadership of the side was similarly lacking in fulfilment. He was fitted for the job, but in fairness to him Lancashire cricket was undergoing a great change in the middle to late 30s. The majority of the great players of the Green-Eckersley era had retired. A new Lancashire was being built, and in that process of building up many of the old traditions went overboard. Some of the younger newcomers refused to accept them. Rightly or wrongly the older professionals felt that something had gone out of Lancashire cricket. Perhaps they were proved right as it would be 30 years before another trophy would be lifted.

Debut at Fenners

In 1923 the story could have ended before it began. Peter was chosen to make his debut for Lancashire whilst at Cambridge against the University. Watching from their car on the boundary were his mother, father and sister. He had been coached by the Lancashire professionals during the winter who saw him as a promising batsman. As the *Manchester Evening News* reported:

> *One had to feel sorry for this cricketer. Having just gone up to Trinity College, Cambridge from Rugby, he had the honour of playing for his county. His one innings didn't trouble the scorers but Lancashire were loyal to him and believed that one day he would make a county batsman and also lead the Red Rose eleven into the field.*

Peter had played for the Lancashire Second XI in 1922 against Durham at Blackpool, scoring 22 & 0. In 1923 he played in five second XI matches but didn't set the world alight, with a top score of 19 not out in nine innings.

Also making his debut for Lancashire in 1923 was George Duckworth, who would go on to be Lancashire's finest wicket-keeper and to take part in Lancashire's five championship wins between 1926 and 1934.

A 21-year-old Peter Eckersley hints at great things to come.

NB: One interesting tradition was that when in winning those championships there was always a George in the side.(George Duckworth). When Duckworth retired Winston Place was given the nickname George and when he retired it was passed to the young Brian Statham.

Learning from the colonel

After the inauspicious start against Cambridge, Peter played just two matches in 1924 against Sussex and Kent where he made a top score of 32*. Lancashire finished fourth in the County Championship. He also played in eleven matches for the Second Xl with one century against Cheshire at Crewe.

1925 saw him play ten matches in the County Championship, averaging 20 with a top score of 82* against Northants at Old Trafford. *Wisden* notes that he batted admirably for three hours and saw a distinct improvement in his batting. Lancashire, again under Jack Sharp, finished third and at the age of 47 decided it was time to retire.

1926 saw the promotion of Col. Leonard Green as captain and Ted McDonald bowled Lancashire to the County Championship with 175 wickets. Peter Eckersley made some useful contributions in his 14 matches and scored 355 runs with a top score of 99.

Also in 1926 Peter was the adopted Conservative candidate for Westhoughton but stood down in early 1927 when he realised that if he was elected his duties as a Member of Parliament would demand more time than he was able to give.

Against Hampshire at Bournemouth, Lancashire found themselves 100 behind on first innings. Eckersley, in partnership with Charlie Hallows, pulled the game around and Iddon and McDonald followed with deadly bowling on a damaged pitch to complete a remarkable transformation. Eckersley was stumped one short of his century in a gallant effort to reach his hundred, but his innings of 99 was in the circumstances twice its face value.

1927 saw Lancashire retain the County Championship, this time with the help of solid batting and the number of first innings points accumulated. This was Peter Eckersley's best season with the bat. Fresh from the M.C.C.

tour to India he scored 600 runs with one century and averaged 29.10. *The Cricketer* noted: *"He is a young player of possibilities. He times the ball well and is probably the most attractive batsman in the side."* His one and only century was made at Bristol against Gloucestershire. Batting with much enterprise he had the distinction of reaching his hundred with the last man in and finishing not out. Let Neville Cardus tell the story:

> *Eckersley had the joy of scoring his first hundred in county cricket; the innings contained much merit, yet cannot compare with the brave piece of cricket he achieved at Bournemouth against Hampshire last year. Obviously, he is full of the true stuff of the game: let us hope he wil go forward according to his essential instincts. There is a most winning enthusiasm about Eckersley and it would be a pity if the unlovely grind of championship machinery were to turn his energy, dull and blunt. Eckersley was pleasantly vigorous as he got near to his hundred, which he reached after just under three hours changeable activity. He plays well to the on, but he must try to get his left foot to the ball in his off-side strokes.*

Eckersley made a valuable 73* not out against Kent at Maidstone to hold the Lancashire innings together and save the follow-on. The report by Neville Cardus in the *Guardian* takes issue with the way Lancashire were playing their cricket.

> *Is the County Championship worth winning at all if the price paid means that in counties like Kent Lancashire come into the reputation of a dull, unadventurous eleven?*
>
> *As I walked around the field today and looked upon the trees, the white tents and the sunlit grass, and as I listened to the band playing happy music, I said to myself "Well here is Lancashire mocking the June setting by slow cricket, and yet they are not doing too well despite all their canniness. If they played a bolder game they could only lose, and how better for the county's ancient name if they went down fighting with a charming gesture." But I am afraid these meditations of mine will be deemed incurably quixotic and old-fashioned at Old Trafford and in other interested places.*

1928 was the last season that Col. Green captained the side and Lancashire were imperious, winning 15 of their 30 games and taking first-innings points in nine of the others. Ernest Tyldesley amassed over 3,000 runs and Charlie Hallows became the first and only Lancashire player to score a thousand runs by the end of May. Watson, Iddon and Makepeace all scored 1,000 runs and Ted McDonald took an amazing 178 wickets at an average of 19.34. They won the county championship by a percentage of 7.92.

A pose for the camera.

Peter didn't play in 1928. He went through an operation at a Manchester nursing home which, although successful, left him very weak. He sustained the injury when touring the West Indies the previous winter, though he was at Old Trafford and practised on the opening day. It was thought advisable not to delay the operation for appendicitis any longer.

Also in 1928 he became the prospective Conservative candidate for the Newton Division of Lancashire. Politics and being an MP was always a great pull for Peter. He was at the time involved running his father's business as well as hoping to forge a cricket career.

As Lancashire celebrated their third successive County Championship at the end of the 1928 season dinner Sir Edward Stockton, Lancashire's President, announced with some regret the resignation of Leonard Green from the captaincy and Lancashire team. Sir Edwin paid a tribute to Lt-Colonel Green's magnificent services during the three years of his captaincy.

We have tried and tried to discuss this matter so that Col. Green need not resign, but he finds his business needs him. He thinks it is time for him to hand over the reins to someone else. The committee, largely with the help of Colonel Green, have been able to get a good substitute. We have decided to ask Mr Peter Eckersley to take the vacant position.

Mr Eckersley said to a *Daily Express* representative: *"I shall accept the position. I shall be very proud to do so, and shall endeavour to fill it as well as my predecessors."* It can only be imagined what Peter Eckersley was actually thinking. His flirtation with standing for Parliament would have led him down a very different road if he had been elected, but he always recognised when he was needed and his desire to serve Lancashire cricket at this time was paramount to him. But what big boots he would have to fill, a hat-trick of County Championship wins under Colonel Green, a strong independent team of professionals. It would take a strong captain and one with immense talents of leadership to take on this role.

Eric Midwinter in his book *Red Roses Crest the Caps* speaks of the Lancashire professional cricketers of that period:

The professional cricketer was the genuine epitome of the respectable topside of the proletariat. Stable, watchful, complacent and a little self-satisfied, they knew their place and preferred it. They were tradesmen, skilled and decently paid. They would stroll, in their good boots, watch chains across their waistcoats, around the wintry streets of their spinning or weaving homelands, unpressurised by the stress of the mill hooter and admired by their peers. In summer evenings they would sink their pints and smoke their pipes in the quiet, second-grade hotels of Worcester or Canterbury, and then, off again by train, to Taunton or to Gloucester. The motor car, the cinema and the dance hall had not yet exerted their socially magnetic pull.

The Lancashire committee for once had made the right choice and the club would be in safe hands under Peter Thorp Eckersley.

3.

Leadership

"The greatest leader is not necessarily the one who does the greatest things. He is the one that gets the people to do the greatest things."
Ronald Reagan

Lancashire were about to make history as the first club to fly to away games, piloted by their new skipper.

IN 1929, AT the tender age of twenty-five, Peter Eckersley was given the Lancashire captaincy. He took over a very successful team of experienced, hardened professionals who had won the County Championship three years running. How would they take to this young amateur being appointed captain to take the team forward? He had nothing to worry about as they respected their new captain, different in style to Colonel Green but one who would maintain the success of the team and deliver another two County Championships.

Eckersley's captaincy did not start well in 1929 with three defeats in the first twelve matches, but things improved in the second half of the season with seven wins from 16 matches and Lancashire finished second to Yorkshire. The batting was held together by Frank Watson with over 2,000 runs but the bowling relied too much on McDonald and Dick Tyldesley. Peter contributed 440 runs with two fifties and a highest score of 78 not out in an hour and three quarters against the South Africans.

Two outstanding performances came against Lancashire that year with two bowlers achieving the rare feat of all ten wickets in an innings: Gubby Allen taking 10-40 at Lord's despite a century from Ernest Tyldesley and Tich Freeman taking 10-131 at Maidstone late in July for Kent, who were leading the championship, although Lancashire still won comfortably by 189 runs.

Surprisingly in 1929 Sydney Barnes played for the Minor Counties at Old Trafford and at the age of 53 bowled for over after over and was still taking wickets!

The Lancashire yearbook prophetically commented on the 1929 season:

Mr Eckersley was not obtrusive as captain, but further experience may suggest greater dominance: in the field he set a capital example.

It also went on to prophesy that:

There is absolutely no reason why Lancashire should not regain the County Championship in the present season. He has done well considering his absence from first-class cricket the whole of the 1928 season after an operation on his return from Tennyson's West Indies Tour of 1927-28. He was a popular captain, winning the respect of his team.

1930 - County Champions

In only Peter's second year of captaincy Lancashire once more won the County Championship, this time going through the whole season undefeated. That displayed the pragmatic attitude of both the captain and the team. There was no pandering to public taste, no desire to play attractive cricket, no attention to anything except the one goal to be attained, to win the County Championship, and they had the good fortune to be able to play the same eleven most of the summer.

They started the season well with two wins and first innings points and in the first seven matches they had five wins. Draws followed and when Kent, the championship leaders, arrived at Old Trafford in July Lancashire asserted themselves to such a degree that victory was won by an innings and 49 runs. A hat-trick by McDonald was the feature of the next victory at Edgbaston, with Eckersley scored a superb 86. As Cardus commented:

Eckersley endeared himself to the Edgbaston crowd by giving them cricket at last that was worthy of the match's bright setting. In a hundred minutes he shook 83 sparkling runs out of a harried and much-manoeuvred attack before forfeiting his wicket by striking across the second ball sent down by the eighth bowler tried.

In the return match Warwickshire narrowly avoided defeat despite Ernest Tyldesley hitting 256 mot out, the highest score of his career. This was the beginning of eight drawn games - rain following the team wherever they travelled - and Yorkshire went to the head of the table at the end of July.

A close race for the championship now developed, eventually won by Eckersley's men as a result of three victories in their last five fixtures. Brilliant bowling by Richard Tyldesley earned himself 12 wickets for 64 in an easy win at Leicester and splendid all-round work gained a second success over Kent at Dover. Two drawn games followed and then the side entered on their last engagement against Essex at Blackpool knowing that outright victory would give them the championship irrespective of what Gloucestershire or Yorkshire could accomplish. Consistent batting led by Watson and Paynter was followed by keen fielding and steady bowling that well earned a winning margin of 174 runs quite early on the third day.

Peter Eckersley averaged nearly 30, scoring 855 runs and playing some very valuable innings. His tactical awareness came to the fore as the county set out to avoid defeat in vital matches, going all out for victory against the weaker teams.

The 1930 championship-winning team.

The Lancashire yearbook commented:

Gustave Dore once painted a neophyte looking at the grizzly monks around him and obviously wondering if he would grow like them. So, I can imagine Mr. Peter Eckersley, a gallant, hard-hitting run-getter, wondering whether in time he will adopt the cautious careful characteristics of his companions. Marriage, brevity of tenure of captaincy, and a certain joy in the game, make the prospect unlikely. But as a vigilant and effective leader he was impregnated with over-doing the safety-first principle, notably at Worcester and Bournemouth. In the latter case there was ample time to make the runs, but he remained content with the points and the game frittered out.

Peter was learning and gaining confidence as captain and this is how he sought to play to win the County Championship. The team that won the title three years in a row were getting older and the 'heavy brigade' was about to break up. Replacing them would not be easy and it would not be for another four seasons before the title would return to Old Trafford.

Also in 1930 Lancashire played Australia (including Don Bradman) at Aigburth. The *Manchester Evening News* report on Friday 16th May titled it 'Eckersley's Match':

The Australians got Lancashire out today for 165, and were left to get 227 to win at the rate of 85 runs per hour. Eckersley, whose batting had been the great feature of the match, was not out 22. His partner, Paynter, was 15 when play started. Eckersley was in good form, as he has been all through the match. He played Grimmett with more assurance than any batsman has shown during the tour. Duckworth came in, but a few runs later Eckersley's excellent innings was closed by an easy return catch to Hornibrook. What batting success Lancashire has had in this match is solely down to Eckersley, who made top score in each innings. But it was not only the 92 (54 & 38) runs which he made in the match that were so useful as the valuable lesson he must have given his own side in proving that the bowling, however good, loses half its terrors if it is attacked with resolution.

Three Fallow Seasons

Losing the first three matches of the 1931 season did not bode well and, although they didn't lose again till the beginning of July, it was too much to catch up. A lot of matches during the season could not be finished with eleven of their fourteen home matches being interfered with by rain. They were also affected by Watson, usually such a consistent run-getter, who was struck down with pneumonia and McDonald, who was not as effective as he used to be. There would be a further blow at the end of the season when Richard Tyldesley, such a reliable wicket-taker, fell out with the club over his contract and he would not play for Lancashire again. He had taken 116 wickets in 1931 at an average of 15.97.

Perhaps the disappointment of the 1931 season and finishing sixth was the reason Peter unsuccessfully contested the Leigh constituency for Parliament. If he had won the seat, he certainly would have had to resign the captaincy, but Parliament's loss was Lancashire's gain.

Campaigning in Leigh during the 1931 election.

1932 saw the Lancashire team in transition. Ernest Tyldesley could be relied upon and he scored over 2,000 runs. Watson weighed in with 1,500 and the young Eddie Paynter and Jack Iddon began to blossom. Sibbles and Iddon had to carry the bowling, taking 200 wickets between them.

Lancashire had a good start to the season, winning three of their first four fixtures including beating Yorkshire by an innings at Bradford. Peter Eckersley led the team well but was hampered by a lack of quality in depth to challenge for the championship. Particularly concerning was the lack of a consistent opening partnership, only once was a hundred run partnership recorded.

Eckersley leads Lancashire out for the game against Kent at Old Trafford in May 1932.

A.W. Ledbrooke, the cricket reporter who travelled with the Lancashire team, had this to say about the Lancashire captain:

Travelling the country with the Lancashire cricket team I became the friend and admirer of Peter Eckersley. His tact and his boyish capacity for friendship endeared him to the Lancashire team and he proved a highly successful captain in spite of the many changes which the Lancashire XI underwent during his period of office.

Never quite a first-class bat, he had the courage to realise his own limitations as a cricketer and the good sense to concentrate on that branch of captaincy which counts for so much - keeping the side together and settling any little squabbles.

At mid-off he was a plucky fieldsman and would attempt to stop the hottest drive. He was full of courage.

He led the team for seven consecutive seasons, during which they twice won the championship, were once runners-up and never finished lower than sixth in the table.

There was a sharp contrast between their two championship wins under his command in 1930 and 1934. In the former year they had Dick Tyldesley and Ted McDonald as their leading bowlers: and Hallows was still a great batsman.

By 1934 those three had dropped out and it was only by magnificent team spirit that the side was reconstructed and brought to such a degree of efficiency.

In 1933 some green shoots started appearing, although the team managed to finish only 5th. They had only one defeat in the championship, succumbing to Yorkshire, but they won nine matches.

The batting held its own and if the criticism of the past was the batting at times, this could not be said of the side in 1933. Lancashire averaged forty runs per wicket - something which no other county approached. The run rate was at times exhilarating with several players scoring over 1,000 runs. The promising debuts of Lionel Lister and Cyril Washbrook would bode well for the future.

That no bowler took 100 wickets was perhaps the difference and the moderate bowling attack meant that Lancashire had to be content with finishing one place higher than the previous year. Peter himself scored 620 runs in 31 matches with an ave of 22.14.

The yearbook commentated on Peter Eckersley:

Never has the popular Peter Eckersley shown such ability as a captain, cleverly handling his meagre bowling, fielding better than anyone else, and making more than twice as many runs as in 1932. His courageous declarations snatched a victory by seven runs from Hampshire with only five minutes to spare. He had a surprising intuition when he put Watson on to open the bowling against Essex, with the result that the first three batsman were dismissed for 19 runs. If he were only granted one really great bowler, he might again lead his excellent side to the next championship.

1934 - The Championship again

The season of 1934 was more than usually memorable in that for the first time in the history of the club the championships of both the first-class and second-class county competitions were won by the Lancashire elevens in the same summer.

It was also unexpected. Lancashire went into their eighth championship match before they produced their second win. Cardus had written before it:

None of us care twopence about the Championship, certainly not this year, when it is obvious Lancashire cannot possibly win it!

But Peter Eckersley had other ideas and he did care about winning the championship again. For him it was a great success as this was mainly a young side which he had moulded and shaped and developed a style of playing freer and more attractive cricket which was reflected in a capacity to force decisive victories.

There were experienced players like Ernest Tyldesley, Iddon, Hopwood, Watson, Duckworth and Sibbles and the average age of the side who made most appearances was only 28. The all-round fielding of the team was of a high standard, perhaps more effective than during the great years of 1926-28, and the batting remained as strong as ever.

If the bowling lacked a McDonald or a Parkin, it contained something for almost every type of wicket, and six bowlers returned an average of under 23 runs per wicket. It was in fact a team of all-rounders and it broke a long championship tradition of emphasis on the importance of fast bowling.

The general character of the side's advance is shown by the fact they scored 2,500 more runs than their opponents for very nearly 100 fewer wickets. A wicket value of 37.62 as against 23.58. The bowling was better with an average fall in the cost of the opposition wickets of 23.58 instead of 27.33

The 1934 Champions:
Back row: Cyril Washbrook, Len Hopwood, Jack Iddon, Frank Booth, Dick Pollard, Len Parkinson, Buddy Oldfield.
Seated: Eddie Paynter, Ernest Tyldesley, Peter Eckersley (capt.), Lionel Lister, George Duckworth.

The side benefited from the captain's luck with the toss, batting first twenty-four times in the thirty championship fixtures. Perhaps it was Peter's superstition of always carrying his rolled umbrella and tossing with a four-shilling piece. So often Lancashire found themselves in a strong position that there were eighteen declarations and the impression was that there was a keen set of players, led with tact and understanding, thoroughly deserving of their unexpected triumph.

Probably the best victory of the season was at Trent Bridge when they were behind on first innings by 147 and recovered so brilliantly that Peter Eckersley was able to declare and force an unexpected triumph.

Peter scored 89 against Derbyshire, which Cardus described as follows:

An innings that Eckersley will remember all his life. Attacking the bowling he scored a real captain's innings, one hit to leg was good enough for Hammond.

He received a standing ovation from the Old Trafford crowd as he returned to the pavilion, bowled eleven short of his century to the regret of all.

From the 22nd May Sussex led the championship and it wasn't until the middle of August that Lancashire overhauled them. Once they reached the top they held on with fine tenacity. The last four matches, surprisingly, were all away from Old Trafford at Southend, Dover, Eastbourne and The Oval. All were drawn with Lancashire winning on first innings and they are worth looking at in some detail.

Cardus describes Southend-on-Sea:

Blackpool without the Tower and a little farther south. Why should cricket still be enthroned in the south and dispossessed at Old Trafford? Why should the game still be in full bloom down here in Southend while Old Trafford is vacant and like a field that has given up its summer plants and now is waste and ready for winter's weeds and desolation?

Lancashire played cautiously but led on first innings and as the third day dawned were all out for 235, leaving Essex 248 to win. Dick Pollard had other ideas, taking three quick wickets, and then Essex looked down and out at 54 for 5 until Nicholls, who had earlier taken 7 for 84, came to the rescue. At tea Essex were 105 for 5 with Nicholls (58) and Cutmore (51) well settled. With nearly an hour to go and still requiring 100 runs Duckworth made what looked like an impossible catch to dismiss Nicholls, but Cutmore held out and saved Essex from defeat. Shortly after six o'clock stumps were drawn.

Lancashire went on to the Dover for the cricket festival and CLR James was reporting for the *Guardian*. He was not very pleased with what he saw:

To-day has been a sorry day for Lancashire cricket. Into the sun and gaiety, the tents, summer dresses, and music of the Dover festival the Lancashire team brought a bleak Northern blast which made one long to hide head and disavow the connection.

Lancashire batted slowly, with Watson and Hopwood only scoring 66 before lunch and even the playing of the brass band while the cricket was on didn't seem to improve the tempo. James at his best describes the day:

The Dover ground is one of the most beautiful in England and was it its best; flag-topped tents to either side of the sleek, green turf, a belt of trees and rows of houses shading into the rolling downs and surrounding the pavilion, high rising terrace after terrace dotted with people looking lazily on and talking of Woolley. The ancient Athenians had terraced seats in the open air, and if they looked at Aeschylus and Sophocles - they had their Olympic Games too. What would an Athenian have thought of the day's play? Probably that the white-flannelled actors moving so sedately from place to place were performing the funeral rites over the corpse of a hero buried between the wickets. Watson and Iddon, from their garb and movements, he would have supposed to be the priests waving the sacrificial wands with solemn dignity.

Watson reached his century before the close as Eckersley joined him and Lancashire had batted all day for 268 for 6.

On the following day Watson was out for 145 made in seven hours. Eckersley forced the pace, hitting his way to 91 in a little over two hours, delighting the crowd with his strokes and hitting thirteen fours.

Lancashire quickly made inroads into the Kent batting, who were 66 for 5 before Chalk and Davies made a fine stand and enabled Kent to come within 70 of the Lancashire score with Phillipson taking 8-100.

To win the match, Lancashire would have to score quickly on the final day. They were 100 ahead when play began. But Watson and Hopwood had other ideas and Lancashire were not going to give anything away. Paynter scored 51 in forty minutes to enliven the day but when the declaration came, it was too much.

Let CLR James have the final word:

A sparkling sun shone down on the beautiful ground as the match trailed its predestined way into futility through a deepening atmosphere of frustration and waste. Lister and Ernest Tyldesley must have been the only persons sorry when the drawing of stumps at four o'clock cut short their bowling.

Top of the table battle

Lancashire went to Eastbourne to play Sussex in a top of the table battle with the sides sitting first and second. Lancashire won the toss and batted, after a short rain delay. Maurice Tate was in magnificent form and the Sussex fielding excellent. Lancashire had a fight on their hands. At 63-3 Ernest Tyldesley held firm with help from Paynter, and despite Tate taking 6-47 Lancashire were in a good place at 190 for 7 with Tyldesley 78 not out.

Rain fell heavily during the night and the Lancashire innings was polished off quickly. The Sussex innings began at 12 o'clock and off Booth's second ball there was a curious 'incident'.

Parks snicked the ball and Duckworth appealed; Parks, who seemed to think he was out, continued to walk up the pitch, but, on realising the umpire had not given him out, began to walk back to his crease; Duckworth came hurrying up to the wicket. Parks now hastened to get in, but Duckworth broke the wicket, and Parks had to go.

At 26 for 3 Lancashire had the start they wanted. Lunch was taken at 57 for 5 and with the sun shining the crowds poured into the ground with the excited crowd hoping that Sussex could retrieve the situation. Eckersley used the bowlers well to suit the conditions, changing them frequently and with judgement. Eventually Sussex were bowled out 53 runs behind and Lancashire had once again won first innings points.

When Watson and Hopwood opened the innings they were taking no chances, aware of the danger from the Sussex bowling attack. Despite noises from the crowd and then jeers Lancashire held firm and at close were 133 ahead with nine wickets in hand. The feeling was that it was feared Lancashire would stick to the first-innings lead and let everything and everybody else slide.

On the final day Lancashire held tight on to their five points and played resolutely for safety. For them to lose the championship they must lose outright to Surrey and Sussex must beat Yorkshire. Lancashire were proving that they could play pragmatic cricket when the mood suited them and Eckersley declared on the final day, leaving Sussex 375 runs to win in 165 minutes. The afternoon ended in peace and tranquility!

CLR James sums up the feeling of those present:

That Lancashire should decide two hours before the end of the second day's play to freeze out the match has met with a harsh reception. Their reputation in the South is already not good; they would not try for fifteen points in Kent, they would not try for fifteen here, though there were times in both matches when they were reasonably safe against all possibility of losing the five for first innings lead. To-morrow they go the Oval, committed to do everything else except secure a finish, the prognostications of a nightmare of boredom are bitter and sincere. Still, a championship is still a championship, but the only justification from this timidity will be success. Should Surrey defeat Lancashire by any chance, and Sussex beat Yorkshire, not only Sussex, but the whole of the South-coast will chuckle till next season.

Lancashire under the leadership of Peter Eckersley were playing pragmatic and 'no frills' cricket. I wonder if the peculiar fixture list with all four of the final matches being played away from Old Trafford had something to do with it. If some of those had been in Manchester, Lancashire may have played more adventurous cricket.

Neville Cardus returned from Test match duty to report on his beloved county in the final match at the Oval knowing that by avoiding defeat they would win the championship. He too was critical of the strategy:

I am afraid that Lancashire's protective policy at Dover and at Eastbourne has succeeded in losing for the team reputation for spirited cricket gained by thirteen victories. Arguments can be produced justifying the tactics employed by Lancashire, but there are arguments which imply that championship ambitions must be satisfied even at risk, indeed of killing cricket. Old Trafford will do well to congratulate itself that at the season's end other crowds have had to suffer the spectacle of a side of fine cricketers endangering a season's handsome work, all for leadership in a tournament in which Yorkshire have been put out of the running because the backbone of their ability has been playing magnificently for England. Lancashire have incurred criticism from lovers of the game because of a last-minute acquisitiveness, the booty of a championship that this year has possessed no reality.

On a flawless Oval wicket the Lancashire score at tea was 247 for one. But Neville was bored with Lancashire looking safe now for the championship:

The game became tired; a draw was in sight on the first day at five o'clock! Even Ernest Tydlesley's cultured play could not keep us constantly interested. Shortly after five o'clock I left the empty, silent ground. Cricket, I said, is dying; the season is over; the crowds have deserted the game for football. The small company at the Oval was like so many mourners at a funeral.

Suddenly as I left the ground to the hollow echoes, I had an inspiration; I would go to Lord's for the closing hour of the Middlesex and Kent match. And at Lord's I found Woolley delighting a great crowd, with everybody eager and the afternoon as animated as though the time of the year was June. Woolley was glorious, the game was alive and keen and beautiful. The crowd was one of the biggest of the season at Lord's, much bigger than any seen at Old Trafford in a county match all summer – football or no football. The journey from the Oval to Lord's was like a journey from death to vivid life. And neither Middlesex nor Kent is in the running for the county championship. Perhaps the financial executive of the Lancashire County and other clubs will make a note of this fact.

On Day two Lancashire attacked the Surrey bowling with an ease and abandon which made Cardus wonder: *"Why at Dover and Eastbourne they batted without strokes and without consciences?"* Peter Eckersley declared just before lunch and Surrey were quickly 32-4. They recovered in the afternoon sun as Cardus observed:

The sun blessed the gallant cricket with its warmth and mellow light. I decline to believe that football has begun. Time enough for football in the rain and mud and cold of winter. I shall wait upon and serve the cricket season until it abdicates in its own gracious way in the lengthening shadows of the year. No true lover of the game withdraws his allegiance merely because the championship points have been added up. The best kind of cricket is festival cricket, and alas! It is never seen in Lancashire.

At the close of play Surrey finished 42 short of the follow-on with two wickets left.

On the final day Lancashire missed the services of Pollard because of an injured toe and Eckersley with a damaged hand. Lancashire forced Surrey to follow-on in spite of some bold hitting by Garland-Wells. Rain showers meant delays and in a short spell Surrey slipped to 136 for 4. More rain delays meant a finish wasn't possible and at four thirty Fender came in. He appealed against the bad light and that was the end of play and the season. Cardus finished his article:

It is a pity that Old Trafford did not have the opportunity to cheer the champions back to the pavilion. They came from the field this afternoon in silence, but no doubt everybody was looking for his umbrella!

Lancashire's win in 1934 should be put into perspective in the history of the club and its significance. It would be another seventy-seven years before a Lancashire captain would again raise the County Championship trophy as undisputed champions. I find the attitudes of CLR James and Neville Cardus a little strange. They wanted Lancashire to play the flamboyant cricket seen earlier in the season when they had seen the side rise up the championship table to the top. The end of season saw the festival matches on the south coast and perhaps they also wanted festival style cricket!!

I can understand Peter Eckersley and the team wanting none of it. They had fought hard all season to top the table and were not going to give it all away by playing in a style which could throw away the county championship.

The last four matches away in the south must have dismayed the team when they saw the fixture list at the beginning of the season and certainly seems an oddity of organisation.

Approaching those four fixtures must have seemed daunting. One slip and they would allow Sussex to overtake them. They knew going into them that first-innings lead in all the matches would be enough to win the championship. That is what they set out to do and they accomplished it with some style. I find the attitude of Cardus on the penultimate day of the county championship almost an act of betrayal. Leaving the Oval and taking a cab to Lord's to watch Frank Woolley. By all means enjoy the grace and beauty of a Woolley innings, but I wonder if Cardus realised that he would never again see his 'beloved red rose county' lift the championship outright in his lifetime! (He would write and watch Lancashire for another 41 winless seasons with only One-Day trophies to celebrate).

Stephen Chalke comments:

The gap in attitude between the northern and southern clubs is so great in these years, isn't it? League cricket in the north teaches young players to be competitive, to want to win, where there is still this attitude in counties such as Kent, Sussex and Somerset that one should play for fun and not worry about winning trophies. The interesting thing is how Cardus buys into the southern attitude. I can't help feeling that some of this is due to his acquired snobbery. It's as if he is a little ashamed of the toughness of the Lancashire culture in which he was bred.

Footnote

At the end of the season Peter spoke at a cricket dinner in Leeds when Lancashire had taken the championship from Yorkshire. Here is an account from the *Yorkshire Post* which reveals much of Peter's character:

Some people talk about the old enmity between Yorkshire and Lancashire on the cricket field, but I prefer to call it the old friendship which is renewed with each succeeding match.

I enjoy the Yorkshire matches better than any others we play, because each match is keen. When we come here to play, we feel at home. The reception we get here is the same as we get at Old Trafford. We meet the same kind of people, who have the same ideas and who play the same kind of cricket. (It was in 1934 that Yorkshire, severely handicapped by Test calls, lost the championship which they held since they took it from Lancashire in 1931).

If we had the privilege of giving our players to England as you did, and had just lost the championship in such a good cause, we should have been very proud indeed.

Any man who played for Lancashire was prouder of beating Yorkshire in a single match than of winning the championship. There were times during his captaincy when he and his team enjoyed the experience.

There was that memorable game at Park Avenue in 1932 when Paynter scored 152 and Sibbles and Hopwood bowled Yorkshire out for 46; but probably the most memorable Roses game in which I played was at Old Trafford in 1933 when the wicket collapsed in amazing fashion and Macauley (who took a hat-trick) and Verity put Lancashire out for 93 and 92 after Mitchell and Barber had batted finely.

In that game Gordon Hodgson, who shared the Lancashire opening attack, marked the wicket opposite the leg stump at the city end. I sent a note to Brian Sellars the Yorkshire captain suggesting that left-arm bowlers should not be used over the wicket when bowling from the other end, but Sellers replied that what was there was the same for both sides. I chuckled when I heard that, I knew what it meant.

It did make a lot of difference as it turned out for the wicket crumbled enough to cause Verity and Macauley to rejoice, and when the game was over and done with, I was able to say that I was among those who had bagged a pair in a Roses Match. It didn't worry me though I was content to wait to the Bank Holiday Match at Headingly where I scored 26 to help Lancashire to a first innings win.

Always Cheery

A cheery fellow always, was Eckersley. Once when asked what he thought about the proposed new leg-before-wicket law, he said. "I find it easy enough to be out as it is, without being out LBW to off-breaks as well." And once when he was chaffed, as he often was, about his fondness for his umbrella, he said that he had got used to it, being in Manchester so much.

That umbrella went with him to every match Lancashire played. Always it dangled neatly rolled up, from his arm. He carried it to the middle when he inspected the wicket; it was there with him when he made the toss and when he was in Leeds in 1934 to speak at the cricket dinner in November, there it was as usual.

That night when he left the hotel the rain was falling. *"Useful thing that umbrella now"* someone commentated.

"Oh, I never unroll it," said Peter and strode out hatless through the downpour.

Little John
Yorkshire Post
August 14th 1940

1935 - The Final season

Lancashire could not hold onto the County Championship which once more passed into the hands of Yorkshire. But the side finished in 4th position, which under the circumstances was better than expected. The Lancashire team was again under transition and found it difficult to complete the matches where they had advantage on first innings. That they lost to all three counties above them in the final table shows the position was a fair one.

Perhaps Peter's thoughts were on other matters as this would be his last season as captain and player for Lancashire. He played in 30 matches but his highest score was only 36 not out and he scored only 324 runs.

The highlights of the season were the run chases which his captaincy encouraged and which saw victories against Yorkshire, Kent and Surrey. The one which just failed was at Old Trafford against Derbyshire where 320 runs were required and the last wicket fell two minutes before the end with seven runs required.

During the season Peter had the satisfaction of seeing the young players Washbrook, Oldfield, Pollard and Phillipson make progress under his captaincy. The team was marked by both an admirable team spirit and of a never-say-die attitude, especially marked by the run chases at the Oval and Dover.

At the end of the season it was announced with a degree of sadness:

That Peter Eckersley having been returned as Member of Parliament at the General Election in November felt compelled to resign his position as captain and Mr Lionel Lister was invited to succeed him.

Peter hoped that he would still be able to play the odd game but this was not to be. Apart from one appearance in 1936 when he captained the Second XI against Yorkshire at Old Trafford his commitments as a MP prevented him playing for Lancashire again.

A farewell to Lancashire.

4.

Exotic climes

"Travel is fatal to prejudice, bigotry, and narrow-mindedness."
Mark Twain

"A ship in harbor is safe, but that's not what ships were built for."
John A Shedd

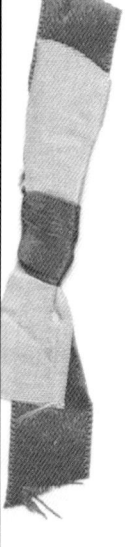

Marylebone
Cricket
Club

Visit to
Madras

Jan.

18

19

21

23

24

25

1927

PETER ECKERSLEY UNDERTOOK three tours to different continents in the 1920s. It may have been thought that it was purely for cricket reasons but in a thoughtful comment in the 1940 *Cricketer* magazine Home Gordon speaks of another reason:

> *People do not realise adequately the educational value of overseas cricket tours. Peter assured me that it was going on the M.C.C. tour of India which gave him adequate perception of the tremendous importance to us of our dominions. He had views on West Indian affairs after going there with Lord Tennyson, whilst he visited Jersey and Guernsey under the leadership of H.D. Swan. Few county captains ever took their responsibility more seriously. When he assumed control of his county team, it contained some unruly elements. With the firm chin below that cheery smile, he won the regard, the devotion and the obedience of all who survived diplomatic selectiveness. He always regarded Duckworth as the man in the field to be consulted.*

M.C.C. tour to India, Burma and Ceylon. 1926-27

The first MCC tour to India since 1902 was very ambitious, with a planned 34 fixtures and all the travelling meaning many of the games were reduced to two-day matches. The team was a strong one captained by A.E.R.Gilligan (Sussex), P.T.Eckersley (Lancs), M.L.Hill (Somerset), G.F.Earle (Somerset), Major R.C.J.Chichester-Constable (Yorks), R.E.S.Wyatt (Warwicks), and the professionals W.E.Astill (Leics), G.S.Boyes (Hants), G.Brown (Hants), J.H.Parsons (Warwicks), A.Sandham (Surrey), G.Geary (Leic), M.W.Tate (Sussex) and J.Mercer (Glamorgan).

In a letter from Lord Harris to the Indian Cricket Board before the tour he talks about the difficulty of the star players Hobbs, Sutcliffe, Hendren, Woolley and Kilner not being available for the tour. He also mentions that on the tour there is to be *'no distinction between amateurs and professionals.'* (see Appendix 1). In further letters Lord Harris worried about the cost of the tour with having to pay the professionals £300 each and the costs of travelling. He also writes about the seven professionals:

In the Republic of Cricket, we rely on these trips to make no distinction of class, they travel and live together and in Australia and the West Indies hospitality is extended to all alike. It is not quite the same in South Africa and on occasions the amateurs have declined invitations because the professionals could not be included, and that is the point about which I feel some concern and as to which I trouble you with this.

I venture to suggest it would be better to avoid invitations which cannot include the professionals(at the military stations) rather than put Gilligan in the unpleasant position of begging to be excused. I am sure you will realise that I only venture to offer opinion at all in the hope that a previous warning may obviate anything that might savor of rudeness or ingratitude on the part of the team.

He does add rather condescendingly, *"The professionals are a well-behaved lot!"* This seems rather strange when in England, Lord Harris and the MCC were observing the very strict code of the difference between amateurs and professionals. Almost forty years later, when the sensitive division between amateurs and professionals still prevailed, a loudspeaker announcement at Lord's informed the purchasers of scorecards that they should amend one entry: *"For F. J. Titmus please read Titmus, FJ."*

The team sailed from Tilbury on 24th September in the S.S.Narcunda calling at Marseilles and Port Said before reaching Karachi.

Being only of two-day duration the first three games were drawn, though the tourists were well placed in each of them. Further matches were played at Rawalpindi and Lahore with Eckersley making his top score of the tour, 86 against The Europeans.

Peter, always the one for adventure, went with Mervyn Hill up country to Rajpipla for a spot of shooting. They were entertained by the Maharaja of Rajpipla. He had won the Irish Derby with his horse Embargo in 1926 and would go on to win the Derby in 1934 with Windsor Lad. Mervyn Hill wrote to his family an account of the expedition:

Just back from Rajpipla. We had a wonderful time. We exercised the Maharaja's polo ponies and watched polo. On Sunday, news came of a kill, so Peter and I sat out and waited over this kill for three hours, but no panther came. It was most exciting. The trouble was that he had eaten so much the night before that he did not mind if he came or not. As a matter of fact, he did come-an hour after we left, but his Highness was waiting at the Palace to give us dinner, so we could not wait. As it was 10-40 p.m. when we sat down to dinner.

As we had failed to kill that night. His highness arranged a drive for us on Monday. We started off at eight o'clock. The train was scheduled to leave at seven, but it was more that the guard's life was worth to start without us. His highness was trying a murder case, so he could not be with us.

We went down the line towards Ankleshwar about twenty miles taking a huge staff with us and a Ford car, which was in due course taken off the train. We then motored three miles to a shooting box in the middle of the jungle. Quite a splendid affair. His highness had it built last year. Then we had breakfast with the O.C. Rajpipla troops which consist of one company of infantry and twenty cavalry and an A.D.C. both of them Indians who had been at Rugby, one of them with Peter Eckersley. After breakfast we saw the bearers-between 1,200 and 1,500 of them -going past to their places. Every native in the place armed with the sticks and staves, bill-hooks and all sorts of murderous weapons. All this for Peter and myself to kill a panther! We then set off with our shikari-who had seen more than two hundred tigers killed-in the Ford for our places.

We had each our own 'machan' which was about two hundred yards distant from the other in jungle that looked rather like chestnut coppice. The grass had been burnt in patches in front, but not behind us, Peter was placed on my right, and between the two of us, also up trees were some boys whose business it was to turn the panther if he came between us. It really was wonderfully exciting when they started beating. The noise was uncanny. I think I had been handed a .303 which though not very heavy had a slightly crocked foresight. After the beat had been in progress for a little over ten minutes and nothing had appeared, my hopes began to rise, for I had been given to understand that the more respectable of the jungle folk move out when a panther enters their part of the forest.

Presently an enormous panther came trotting out, about seventy yards from me among the trees. He turned his head my way, offering an easy shot. Aiming to just miss the head, I fired and hit him in the shoulder The beast gave a great grunt, jumped three feet in the air, turning complete summersault and recovering dashed past me in the jungle behind us. I arranged to fire off a couple more shots at him, but they were only chance ones. I was quite convinced he would not get far, and as the beaters were coming closer. I was beginning to think that the show was just about over when all of a sudden, I saw another panther moving in front of Peter. Something must have frightened her, for she suddenly turned and passed me at the gallop, presenting a perfect broadside shot nearly seventy or eighty yards away. I fired as though I were using a shotgun and hit her right through the shoulder. She turned three summersaults rather like a rabbit and then lay dead. Never have I been so thrilled in my life.

After this we got back into the Ford car and went for lunch, while the shikari went off to see what he could find in the way of tracks. The jungle into which the panther had gone was fairly thick and divided by a river. But this was dry which made it quite easy to see if he had crossed. They reported back to us that he was still out there in the jungle so when we had finished our lunch, we organized another smaller beat to try and flush him out.

Peter and I positioned ourselves on the same side of the river but only forty yards apart. Peter not realizing how close we were to each other. Presently the panther appeared directly opposite me, offering me a beautiful broadside shot, but just as I had him in my sights Peter loosed off a shot which went wide. I could not help myself and I too pulled at the trigger and missed. The animal crossed the river and dashed into the undergrowth behind us. I managed to get in a couple more shots and Peter at least one but I fancy we can have done little more damage to him.

We left them tracing the beast. Dashed bad luck that, Peter firing when he did, for the panther would have been an easy shot for me. I still can't fathom how, though when my first shot must have hit its mark and all the evidence pointing to his going lame, he did not give the appearance of having being badly wounded.

The Times of India on 16th December 1926 reported:

M.C.C. PLAYERS AS HUNTERS
ECKERSLEY AND HILL AS BIG GAME SHOTS

P.T. Eckersley and M.L. Hill, two members of the M.C.C., took advantage of the fact they were not playing against Bombay Presidency to take a holiday from the cricket field and journey to Rajpipla for a big game shoot. Each was lucky enough to get a panther and they are naturally pleased with themselves at their success.

Hill had particular cause for satisfaction as the shot which enabled him to get his first big game trophy was one worthy of the great Selous himself. The wicket-keeper after missing the beast when it was standing still, bowled him over while he was running away, the distance being quite a hundred yards, the panther being killed on the spot.

The players were the recipients of numerous congratulations on being fortunate enough to get a panther-enough for their first innings.

Mervyn Hill wrote a diary during the tour and here is an excerpt:

In January the tour sailed to Madras where they were entertained regally at the Adyar club where dancing and free champagne all night had an effect on them the following day. Some of the party went on a snipe shoot followed by a garden party at Government House.

There was much entertaining with a day at the races. We all lunched with the Stewards and a dammed good lunch it was too. All imported in cold storage from England. Good old beef-pheasant-salmon and even English butter. In the evening they attended a show when the team were invited to go on stage and be presented with silver mugs.

Against a team called 'All Madras' Peter Eckersley scored a brisk 47 before being out leg before wicket. In the evening the team attended a play given in their honour. The Madras Dramatic Society presented 'How's', which can best be described as incense burnt in the honour of cricket and the Marylebone Cricket Club. The men's costumes were made Pierrot-fashion in the MCC colours. Wisely as a contrast to this exuberance the ladies were dressed entirely in black and wore wigs. The cricketing atmosphere was continued with a burlesque cricket match in the second half of the show with songs and pantomime.

MCC played the Europeans which was distinguished with E.A. Cowdrey (father of Colin) scoring 48 for the Europeans. Another unusual feature was Bob Wyatt accepting a bet to ride a motor-cycle around the ground during the interval with a woman's hat on. He accomplished it to the delight of the crowd at a speed of 50mph earning him 30 rupees.

Hill was left out of the last three-day match at the last minute, preventing him going on a really good shoot. *"So here I am down on the ground...watching cricket!!!"* Maurice Tate reached 1,000 runs on the tour and in the same innings had his teeth knocked out by the bowler! Peter Eckersley scored a very valuable 60 not out, including eight boundaries, pulling to leg with refreshing vigour.

Arthur Gilligan was interviewed by *The Hindu* paper saying that Madras had been most hospitable. He also said the Madras weather had been kind to them after the first few days, adding laughingly, *"Your mosquitos have scored more runs, taken more wickets, and caught more catches than all our flannelled opponents together."*

In Maurice Tate's *My Cricketing Reminiscences*, he wrote:

We took the train through Southern India, with its impenetrable jungles, and across the dreaded Palk Straight to Ceylon. Like the trip from Australia to

Tasmania this lived up to its reputation for roughness. The boat tossed like a cockle-shell and the smell of decaying fish added to the horrors of the voyage.

According to *The Times of India* on the way to their port of embarkation members of the team found themselves having to shake hands with everybody at each station they passed through. When the presence of an individual was denied with a *"Not here!"* thinking that the crowd did not know him, he was obliged to shake hands twice as a penalty.

ALONGSIDE

They played three matches in Ceylon with Tate completing the double of 1,000 runs and 100 wickets. Bob Wyatt performed the unusual feat of scoring a century and taking a hat-trick.

When the team returned to India, they played their final matches and incurred their only defeat in almost unusual match against the Delhi Ladies.

Let the *Hindustan Times* tell the story:

The match against the Delhi Ladies was a half-day fixture and was according to a lady spectator 'A scream'.

From start to finish the occasion enabled Brown to excel himself in the role of what Sir Hugh Clifford described in Columbo as the greatest jester in the world, for he appeared in a clown's cap and nose wearing an antique pair of spectacles and the paraphernalia to match. He was the stand-out man in a revel of levity which did not, even for a moment, degenerate into a spirit of unsportsmanlike seriousness and kept the large company of spectators almost shedding tears of laughter.

Peter Eckersley played for the Ladies and even wore a skirt to blend him in with his team. The most interesting feature of the Ladies innings, which produced quite a respectable total of 124 runs, was the remarkable vigorous efforts of Miss P.T. Eckersley whose unladylike swipes while at the wicket gave the tourists much leather hunting, and the latter were heartily glad when the boyish-looking player in skirt and jumper mowed down all three stumps with an agricultural stroke which appeared hardly consistent with "her" previous polished display.

Mercer who was one of the umpires seemed to be interested in some extra-terrestrial object, for whenever an appeal was made for or against the lady players, he was found gazing skyward, and Tate an otherwise excellent fielder fumbled so badly on occasions that in addition to spoiling several chances of getting players run out, he in his hurry prevented good throws from hitting the wicket.

Mrs. Ball who captained the ladies team batted well for an unbeaten 14 but the best contributor to the home total was "Miss Extras" who claimed 32 runs including 23 wides.

Never before were the M.C.C. dogged by such rotten luck as when they went in to bat. Brown, who opened the innings with Sandham wielding the broken stump of a bat, the blade of which was smaller by half than the handle, was almost spitefully run out by Sandham. Boyes and Govan who played for the M.C.C. suffered the same fate being not fleet enough on their feet against the lightning return of the ladies.

Further the handicap of four-stumps wicket seemed to tell heavily against the erstwhile redoubtable English players, for four of them were bowled, at least one of them pulling a widish ball into his wicket. Hill was imprudent enough to jump out at a critical moment and was smartly stumped. Chichester-Constable tried vainly to sustain a lost cause, but Grant Govan running himself out gave him absolutely no chance and the hitherto unbeaten M.C.C. were at last defeated by 55 runs.

There was a popular demonstration at close of play, and the M.C.C. were cheered as they left to catch the special train that was to take them to Patiala.

Reading the accounts of this tour and all the extra activities, the dances, receptions, shows, the big game hunting and the hospitality of the people shows the variety and enjoyment of the pre-war tours. Also, it gave the touring team the ability to mix with the local population and see the country for themselves, with the long sea trips providing the time to relax and have fun.

It's pertinent to compare these tours of nearly 100 years ago with present tours where players fly into and from drab airports to hotels and then are escorted to the grounds, sometimes with armed guards. Their relaxation is taken in hotel rooms which could be anywhere with the TV screen for comfort. The tours seem so different and you see from the reports how 100 years ago, despite the arduous travelling, as well as the cricket they had so much fun.

But trouble was brewing though in the form of complaints being written to Lord Harris and the M.C.C. from India. After the team had been there the

Governor in Bombay congratulated the tourists on the way they played cricket and how they took part in the social engagements, but he did raise a concern:

> *The real fact is that it is quite impossible for a team to tour India, play cricket and at the same time attempt to carry out the mass of social engagements expected of them. Frankly, between ourselves, Gilligan was getting quite nervy, and I took it upon myself to take him aside one night and give him a real lecture on the subject. Telling him it was not fair, either to himself, to the M.C.C. team or to cricket to endeavor to do all they were doing, and that he must put his foot firmly down about these social engagements. He quite frankly realized that what I said was true, and promised me faithfully-and, in fact, has already written to Calcutta to say that, when they are there, the team is never to stay up at night at any engagement after 11pm, and that on days they are not playing cricket, they will have up to lunch-time entirely slack and without engagements, so as to get a real rest. I am really anxious about them, as several of the team themselves realize that it is impossible to continue at the rate they have been going, and to last the course.*

There are a further series of letters between the Governor of Bombay and Lord Harris about the tour. Lord Harris asks confidentially about the behaviour of Gilligan's team. He replies:

> *There has been a great deal of comment in the Calcutta Press and by individuals on Gilligan's accusation of snobbishness, which of course was directed against Calcutta. I know a good deal about it, and as for myself, I am convinced that the whole fault lay, in the first instance, with the Europeans in Calcutta. If they had only adopted the policy we adopted in Bombay with regard to the Clubs. I do not think that any feeling would have arisen.*

He goes onto say that in his opinion the cricketers were not to blame at all. Further letters raise some minor almost puerile complaints referring to a damaged pillow case and door at a hotel and the mix up about bar receipts and free drinks. There were also comments made about the Indian Railway and the condition of the trains.

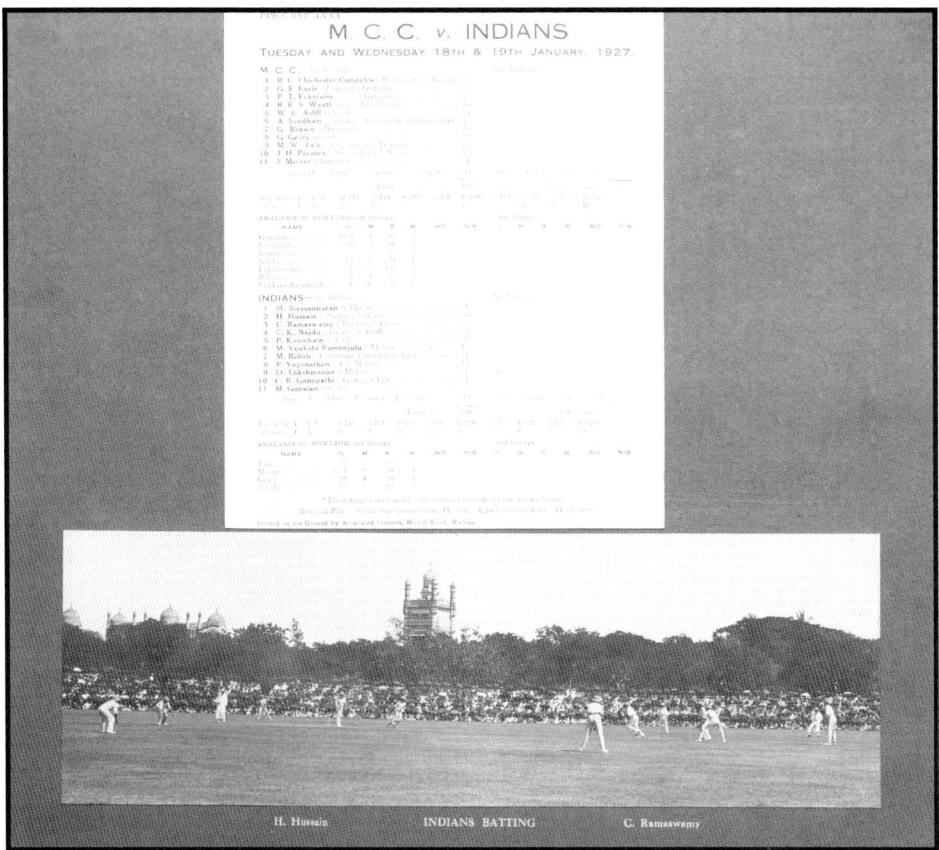

In conclusion it seems that during a long and arduous tour over a large part of India there were bound to be some minor problems and that some people wanted to magnify these. The way in which the touring party was constructed, with a mixture of amateurs and professionals, was perhaps a problem waiting to explode. In England social distinctions were recognised and even policed and enforced by the counties. So it may have seemed strange to a member of the Yacht Club in Bombay and Calcutta when the M.C.C. team arrive and they want to apply their own social order, i.e. only allowing amateurs into the club and not inviting the professionals, that they were castigated for being "snobs". A case perhaps of do what I say and not what I do! (See letters in Appendix).

1928 - Tennyson's Tour to Jamaica

Peter Eckersley went with Hon. Lionel Tennyson on a short tour to Jamaica in the spring of 1928. The party was Hon. L.H.Tennyson(Capt.), T.Arnott, A.L.Hilder, M.J.C.Allom, Col. D.C.Robinson, G.D.Kemp-Welch, F.J.Seabrook, G.J.V.Weigall, P.T.Eckersley, A.K.Judd, and the professionals C.P.Mead, G.M.Lee, D.Sullivan and E.W.Clark.

In his biography of Tennyson, Regency Buck, Alan Edwards describes the tour captain thus:

> *Lord Lionel Tennyson was one of cricket's most colourful characters of the last century. On the field he was a charismatic team captain and hard-hitting batsman with a penchant for smiting sixes, while off the field his exploits would have been a godsend to today's tabloids. With prodigious appetite for the high life, substantial gambling losses and relentless womanising in modern times he would never have been out of the headlines.*

The team travelled in the banana boat *Changuinola* and had a very rough outward journey. It was therefore no surprise that Jamaica won the first match, which began on the second day after arrival. Another surprise was the accommodation and they had to camp with the Argyle and Sutherland Highlanders, the amateurs in the officers' mess and the professionals with the sergeants. They were also asked to play on nineteen of their twenty-three day stay.

The tour was a success for the stalwart Phil Mead, who scored centuries in all three first-class matches and another in a minor game. The tour was particularly historic in that it marked the first-class debut of George Headley. He scored 211 in the third match of the tour and Jamaica won two out of the three matches. Peter Eckersley scored 50 in the final match. Interestingly, on the tour was Maurice Allom, who was later to marry Peter's widow Audrey after Peter was killed in 1940.

Sir Julian Cahn's tour to Argentina 1929/1930

It was no great surprise that for his next tour Peter chose another continent to explore, this time South America. Sir Julian Cahn, a very successful British businessman, philanthropist and cricket enthusiast arranged the tour. Sir Julian was president of both Nottinghamshire and Leicestershire county cricket clubs. He eventually built his own pitch at Stanford Hall so he could watch games from his home.

From 1929 to 1939, Cahn was the captain of his own team, the Sir Julien Cahn XI, that toured the world. It was one of the most successful private teams, losing only 19 out of 621 cricket matches. Cahn recruited top players from outside England, including Australians Vic Jackson and Jack Walsh.

Cahn played in many of his teams' matches, including six of the 13 first-class matches they played between 1929 and 1939. He made his first-class debut in March 1929 at the age of 46 when his team was playing in Jamaica. Stephen Chalke has written:

No English first-class cricketer of the 20th century can have had less ability than Cahn. He was a hypochondriac, often preferring his electric wheelchair to walking ... he batted in special inflatable pads that it was his chauffeur's duty to pump up.

The team sailed from Tilbury on February 20th in the *Avolena Star* bound for Buenos Aires. As well as the cricketers Sir Julian took his wife, maid and personal barber as well as other members of his family with the party numbering 30 in total. The cricketers were F.W.H. Nicholas, F.C.W. Newman, T. Arnott, L. Green, P.T. Eckersley, H.R. Munt, R.W.V. Robins, H.R.S. Critchley-Salmonson, G.F.H. Hearne, S.D. Rhodes, C.W. Flood, C.A. Rowland, J.R. Gunn, T.L. Richmond and H.D. Swan.

The Atlantic crossing was smooth with delightful weather. Many different sports were organised by the crew and when the ship crossed the equator many of the cricketers had to pay the usual tribute to Father Neptune, with their immersion in a large tank of water with the ship's captain acting as Neptune. There were also many social events with dances and revues.

When they arrived in Buenos Aires the team were treated as VIPs and cricket emissaries and greeted by the most senior dignitaries and representatives of the British Empire. They practised at the Belgrano Ground and the first few days were extremely hot with even Sir Julian, who never ventured out without his layers of sweaters, stripped down to his shirtsleeves.

In all six matches were played, but the ones of importance were the three 'tests' against Argentina. Cahn's XI won the first and the remaining two were drawn with Peter Eckersley scoring 88 in the third 'Test'. They were impressed with the high standard of cricket in the Argentine and in particular the excellent cricket grounds.

The team were shown great hospitality off the field with high spirited dinner dances. On the days they were not playing cricket they visited places of interest, including the largest chilled meat factory in the world.

On the return journey they docked at Santos and they journeyed by car to Sao Paulo where they visited the cricket ground and were intrigued by the huge sightscreens that had been erected in order to prevent the stoppage of play by the frequent passing trains. On the voyage back to England very, rough seas were encountered in the Bay of Biscay and they were all pleased to see Plymouth on the 23rd April.

Other tours

Peter also undertook other cricket tours to Europe, notably with the Free Foresters to Holland in 1937. R.A. Boddington, the Lancashire player, was captain and in the first match at The Hague against a Netherlands XI they were 184 for 6 overnight with Eckersley not out. The report says that *"An evening dancing at a Russian Restaurant proved a good stimulant for Eckersley who went on to make 86."* The Foresters went on to win by 10 wickets.

The second match was against The Flamingo's at Lahurn followed by *"A tour of the local night clubs where much drinking was enjoyed and it was a good job there was no cricket the following day."*

He also went with an M.C.C. team to Jersey and Guernsey in the 1920s under the leadership of H.D. Swan, described by E.W. Swanton as one of the worst cricketers he had ever seen. However, he was influential at Lord's and organised tours to Jersey and Guernsey for the M.C.C. from 1924 until 1939. H.D. Swan was always captain, usually batting at no 11 and not troubling the scorers very much and being described as ponderous and pompous.

At a cricket lunch Sir Julian Cahn played an amusing trick on him. Swann had just stood up and thanked the directors of a shipping firm, Elders and Fyffe, whose team they were playing, for their hospitality and the way they transport cricket teams across the seas to strengthen the bonds of empire. As the discourse ended Sir Julian slipped a whoopee cushion on his chair. Swann sat down to a deep echoing reverberation and startled looks around the room only broken by Sir Julian's laughter revealing the joke.

In 1924, on the first tour to Jersey with Duleepsinjhi and other notables in the team, Peter scored 18 and 14. The following year there was rough weather on the journey to Guernsey and several members of the team suffered severely from the effects of the 'mal-de-mar'. They played on the Elizabeth College ground followed by a dance at the governor's house. In the match against Jersey, Peter top scored with 38 and 125.

There was also a tour to Portugal in 1934 with family and friends. Lionel Tennyson came along with other cricketers and they played two matches at Lisbon and Vigo. There are many photographs in the family album.

One of the very last games of cricket Peter played was in August of 1937 when he turned out, along with his predecessor as Lancashire captain, Leonard Green, for the Free Foresters against All Holland in Amsterdam.

The Free Foresters in Amsterdam with Peter Eckersley fourth from the right and Leonard Green to his right.

It seemed as if Peter would take every opportunity to participate in a cricket tour, wherever it was. Naturally inquisitive, he took opportunities to learn about other cultures and although cricket was the medium by which this occurred, perhaps there was always in the background the observation made by Home Gordon about the educational benefit of foreign climes and the preparation for a future career in parliament.

5.

Courage

"He who is not courageous enough to take risks will accomplish nothing in life."
Muhammed Ali

With wife Audrey on the Parliament terrace.

AT THE END of the 1934 season Peter Eckersley was chosen to fight the seat of Manchester Exchange for the Conservatives. Situated in the centre of Manchester it was an odd Parliamentary seat in that it had 16,000 voters living outside the boundary. Businessmen, their wives, partners in private companies were registered to vote in Manchester whilst living elsewhere. One of the problems this caused was that when voting took place transport was required to bring in voters from Blackpool, Southport, Knutsford and other residential areas. The *Manchester Evening News* noted:

> *Mr Eckersley has already obtained a polling-day squad of over 200 motor-cars. Some of these will travel 30 or 40 miles to bring back four or five voters. To-morrow his activities will have a distinctly sporting atmosphere, for he is bringing a small army of friends-men well known in local cricket, aviation, rackets and motoring circles.*

Well aware of the rising threat of Italy and Germany at one of the poll meetings he had this to say:

> *On the naval issue, there has never since 1914 been more potent international danger. Military sanctions, as in the Labour policy, would be a dangerous error, Italy would not knuckle under such treatment. Some of our opposition parties favour disarmament. Peace does not at the moment lie through weakness but through continued support of the League with sufficient strength behind us as the greatest member to keep the peace of Europe*

It was also noted that Peter's aviation experience would stand him in good stead:

> *Aviation, in one form or another, has become so important a feature of national life that Mr. Eckersley's first-hand knowledge would undoubtedly be of great value in the House.*

In days when women were supposed to be seen but not heard Audrey Eckersley cut an attractive figure as she canvassed for her husband:

Few men, even, have entered a campaign with the zest Mrs Eckersley is showing in the support of her cricketer-husband in the Exchange Ward. Business men in the division find her knowledge of National affairs the right whetstone for an interesting discussion. For Mrs Eckersley has brains as well as beauty, and confided to a reporter that she takes care to let the voter show in which aspect of politics they are most interested.

The result was an easy victory for Peter Eckersley with a majority of over 7,000 votes and as he accepted victory he spoke at the declaration that he would be retiring from cricket:

I shall resign from the captaincy of the Lancashire team tomorrow morning. I shall do so with great regret. It will mean that I shall be able to play as an amateur in a few matches during my holidays. But if during those periods the new Lancashire Captain will have me. I shall be only too pleased to play again for the old county, providing it does not interfere with my political duties.

Lancashire thanked Peter Eckersley for his captaincy of the club by making a presentation to him and his wife of a silver engraved tray with a silver set of water-jugs. In responding to the presentation, he thanked the club and the committee for their regard for his services, and spoke with warm appreciation of the sportsmanship and the friendliness of the Lancashire crowd at the matches. It was he believed the kindest crowd that could be found in England.

Not only are your young men good cricketers now, but they will become better cricketers. We can view the future with the greatest calm and confidence.

After taking his seat in the House of Commons he quickly made his maiden speech, which was unsurprisingly about flying and raised a great deal of interest. He spoke at length on the air estimates introduced by the Under Secretary for Air, Sir Philip Sassoon, and stressed the need for young men to be taught to fly. "*Young men would be eager to serve in the air, if opportunities were provided, giving more assistance to light aeroplane clubs,"* he said. It would only be five years later that those same young men would help win the Battle of Britain in the skies in their hurricanes and spitfires and many would die, sacrificing their lives for their country.

In the same year he was present at a fund-raising dinner in Manchester to help Jewish children in Germany to be re-settled as the Nazi regime had forbidden Jewish mothers to have Grade A milk along with other strictures.

Cricket was not forgotten and the M.C.C. recognised his qualities when they invited him to be nominated for the M.C.C. selection committee in 1936. Writing in the *Home and Empire* magazine he had this to say about 'Choosing the ideal Captain and picking the Test team'.

The Captain must be chosen early, and it is most important that once picked he should be included in all future deliberations of the Selectin Committee. After all he has got to lead the men on the field and it might be disastrous to present him with a ready-made team.

Captains must be chosen primarily for their knowledge of the strategy of the game, but there are many considerations that must weigh with these who are making the choice. The captain must be a leader of men, able to command their confidence. He should preferably not be a bowler. The reason is, of course, that in most cases the captain who is also a bowler tends to bowl himself too little, simply because he has every opportunity of bowling too much. We have had great bowling captains–Sir Stanley Jackson springs to mind–and we may have them again, but it is one of the things that must be put down on the debit side against a man.

Wicket-keeper is really the best ideal position for a captain, but it is very rarely the best wicket-keeper that is also the best captain. So far as I know, one such was MacGregor, of Middlesex, but that was nearly thirty-five years ago. Failing that, the captain should preferably be first slip or mid-off, for both positions give him the opportunity of seeing the progress of the game as a whole. Incidentally, captains are often better batsmen than their averages suggest, for they are always ready to go in at the most difficult stage of the game and consequently often bat under bad conditions.

He discusses the merits of the players needed to fulfil the positions in the touring side, two fast bowlers, two medium pace and two spin bowlers. In an interesting aside he says that:

Selectors do not, I think, set out with the determination to provide at least one wag in a side. Such a man is invaluable on a long tour, and on the field his jokes sometimes help to break a dangerous tension. The slow bowler who had been hit for fours and sixes all-round the ground in one over. 'Cheer up old man, you've got him in two minds. He doesn't know whether to hit you for four of six.'

Peter spoke at Lancashire's opening luncheon of the 1936 season, saying that:

The side under their new captain Lionel Lister had a team which had the main essentials which any side which was going to win the championship must have. -good fielding!

But a disappointing season saw Lancashire finish 11th despite a splendid final month of the season when they won five matches.

Playing for Lord's & Commons

It was thought that in the 1850s 'all work and no play makes Jack a dull boy' was true and applied to Parliament so in 1850 the Lord's and Commons Cricket Club was founded. It was a real mix of parliamentarians, a sprinkling of Lords as well as members of all parties with the aim of relishing the enjoyment of playing the game.

Peter played four matches between 1935 and 1939, against I Zingari as captain and against the M.C.C., Westminster School and the Parliamentary Staff at the Oval. Against the Parliamentary Staff Peter opened the batting, laying the foundations of the innings with 63. In this match he played alongside Lord Ebbisham, who at the age of 68 astounded the crowd with his agility in the field and bowling, taking 7 for 25. Lord and Lady Ebbisham entertained both teams during and after the match with Luncheon and Tea.

In 1936 Peter surprised the Lancashire members by returning to captain the Colts in the second eleven match against Yorkshire. He prepared for the match by having nets at Lord's.

The new Member of Parliament for Manchester Exchange practises in the nets at Lord's.

During the 1930s Peter and Audrey moved from Lowton House to live at Midways near Bowdon in Cheshire. It was here that their two sons were born, Peter and Roger, and who both went to Eton and played cricket there.

Peter Eckersley played for Bowdon C.C. in the 1930s and was associated with the club for a number of years.

Working as an M.P. to the outbreak of the war

Peter was not only busy in parliament but was a very conscientious constituency M.P., attending meetings and also very involved in fund-raising. He put out an appeal for the Library service at Manchester and Salford hospitals. Over 12,000 books were donated and the initiative was a great success. He was a keen supporter of the White Heather Camps in Heaton Park, where boys from the inner city of Manchester would camp during July learning various outdoor skills. He also presided over a 'Roses' cricket match for the boys in the park. He and his wife were both very popular in the constituency, opening many bazaars and generously giving of their time.

Speaking at the Manchester and District Playing-fields Society, he spoke in relation to the danger of the country turning into a nation of watchers:

The aggressor countries were training their young people to be physically fit because they wanted war. We in this country hoped there would be no war anymore and we were doing our very best to see that there was not. We are not training our young people to be cannon fodder, but to be fit in their bodies and in their minds and therefore happy citizens.

An unusual feature of meeting his constituents was choosing street-corners in his constituency to meet "the man-in-the-street". He did this a number of times and it proved very popular. He remarked:

It did have its lighter side. I was asked by a woman whether I knew of any cleaning jobs and some people even tried to borrow money!

In parliament he was a keen speaker on anything aeronautical. He urged the government to give more assistance to light-aircraft clubs as they would produce the pilots of the future if ever they were needed for a war.

Mr. P. T. ECKERSLEY, M.P.

AN APPRECIATION.

IT is entirely appropriate to place on record that few Members have "broken their duck" in Parliament more successfully and attractively than Mr. P. T. Eckersley, the former captain of the Lancashire County Cricket Club.

His views on the problem of the Air and the eagerness of our air-minded youth to serve if given the chance were very well delivered, and the compliments paid his maiden effort afterwards had more than the usual formal complimentary sincerity.

Sir Philip Sassoon, Parliamentary Under-Secretary for Air—and himself a very fine speaker—was not the least of the admirers of Mr. Eckersley's speech.

The House always enjoys and appreciates the new member who brings something fresh to the Parliamentary stock-pot, and when next the Member for the Exchange Division of Manchester catches the Speaker's eye he will be assured of a good House.

Mr. Eckersley's speech gained considerably in appeal, of course, because of his very practical knowledge of aviation and his strenuous efforts to further the cause of light aeroplane clubs.

Members were recalling to-day his work in this connection, and especially his unremitting work to popularise the 'plane for fulfilling sporting fixtures.

"We can do with members like Eckersley because he knows what he is talking about," was one tribute paid by an old Parliamentary hand.

"Air is bound more and more to become of paramount importance politically, but the number of M.P.'s who are really acquainted practically with the subject is surprisingly small."

There was a visit to Spain along with other M.P.'s to have an audience with General Franco. Showing his impartially he also helped trace the son of a communist constituent who was serving in the International Brigade.

Away from parliament he took time out of his busy schedule to visit Old Trafford during the Australian match in 1938 and "take round the hat" for Len Hopwood's benefit, and for the first time at Leigh Police Court a mother and son sat together on the bench. Peter Eckersley sat with his mother Eva Mary, who was also a J.P.

War clouds gather

Peter was appointed Secretary of the Parliamentary Air Committee and spoke often in the House and also at public meetings about the importance of putting resources into the British Air Force.

He held the view that the best form of defence against aerial attack was to have the most powerful Air Force existing within range of any possible aggressor. He believed it would be a great deterrent to any country contemplating an air attack to know that we had a greater attacking force that could retaliate quickly and effectively.

Peter asked a question in the House of Commons of why certain units of the army had been issued with pyjamas of Japanese manufacture and whether the minister would take immediate steps to see that in future only articles of British manufacture would be issued.

As private secretary to Lloyd George at the Board of Trade he was kept busy in the House of Commons, proving himself to be a tireless and efficient M.P. But as soon as war was declared and despite doctors saying he was unfit for active service he joined the Fleet Air Arm, which provided air cover for shipping.

As an M.P. he need not have served in the Fleet Air Arm as it was regarded as a reserved occupation. But he was anxious to do his duty for his country, for his heart was in flying. His decision showed great courage but did not surprise those who knew Peter Eckersley.

6.

Sacrifice

"Great achievement is usually born of great sacrifice, and is never the result of selfishness."
Napoleon Hill

"The ultimate test of a man's conscience may be his willingness to sacrifice something today for future generations whose words of thanks will not be heard."
Gaylord Nelson

IN AUGUST 1940 Peter was serving as a Lieutenant on 758 Squadron Fleet Air Arm based at H.M.S Raven (the wartime name for Southampton Airport). 758 Squadron was formed from the Observer and Signals School on the 1st July 1939 and flew Osprey, Shark, Skua and Proctor aircraft.

August 1940 was also marked by the start of the Battle of Britain, Goring's heralded 'Eagle Day'.

The Luftwaffe chief, Reichsmarschall Hermann Göring, issued the Adlertag (Eagle Day) directive, a plan of attack in which a few massive blows from the air were to destroy British air power and so open the way for the invasion of Britain.

This intensive phase began on 8th August. The Germans launched bombing raids involving up to 1500 aircraft a day and directed them against the British fighter airfields and radar stations. By late August the Germans had lost more than 600 aircraft and the RAF only 260, but the RAF was rapidly losing badly needed fighters and experienced pilots and its effectiveness was further hampered by the bombing damage done to its radar stations.

One rather strange note is that Goering claimed his planes had sunk HMS Raven, which was of course the name given the Southampton airfield. It was recorded in *Picture Post*.

On the 13th August 1940, when the Battle of Britain was at its height, Eckersley, together with Airman Sidney J Snow, a 19-year-old Air Gunner were flying in a Percival Proctor unarmed training aircraft, No P6113, when it crashed near Winchester. The exact location is Hookpit farm, very close to Worthy Down airfield.

The date of August 13th was auspicious - it was the day that Peter's father William died some seventeen years earlier.

On 13 August 1940, the weather over the Channel was cloudy and dull around dawn. Therefore, Goering postponed operations, but by this time bombers had already taken off and could not be contacted to turn them back. This led to combat over the North Kent Coast, Midhurst and Arundel. With improving weather, further raids occurred in the late morning and early afternoon over Portland. In the late afternoon, around

16:00 to 16:30, the Luftwaffe were in the Portland/Southampton area. Claims as 'probably destroyed' were made in the Winchester area by Pt. T. Grier of 601 Squadron for a Me 110 and by Flt. Off. W.C. Clyde of the same unit for two Me 110s (Luftwaffe records suggest only one Me 110 was shot down near North Baddersley by Hurricanes, another came down in the sea while others returned damaged from the operation). So it would appear the Luftwaffe were in the Winchester area on the day the Proctor crashed, but nothing to suggest they were in any way responsible.

The report from the inquest, which was held at Winchester and presided over by the County Coronor M.A.L. Bowker, reads:

Lieutenant Eckersley, whose home was in Ashley, Cheshire, was M.P. for the Exchange Division of Manchester and for several years captained the Lancashire County Cricket XI. He was aged 36 years. He was piloting a machine on a routine training flight when it crashed and burst into flames. Able-Airman Snow who was aged 19 years was a passenger in the machine. His home was at Oxford Road, Bow, London.

A policeman, P.C. Amery, speaking at the inquest said:

I saw Lieutenant Eckersley's machine turn sharply into a spiral dive and crash from a height of 500ft on to a farm. At the time the engine was turning over slowly. The machine burst into flames and Lieutenant Eckersley, who was the pilot, and Sidney John Snow, aged 19, a qualifying air gunner, were both burned to death. When a witness reached the machine it was burning fiercely and he could not get near it.

A brother officer said that Lieutenant Eckersley had joined the R.N.V.R. last September and had 1200 hours flying experience (more than anyone other pilot at the base). A verdict of accidental death was returned.

Billy Blake, who flew Procters with 756 Squadron at Worthy Down states in a book about to be published:

These Proctors were originally the Percival Vega Gull, a sort of rich man's toy but a thoroughly practical light aircraft. Equipped for blind flying, landing lights and powered by a six-cylinder 200hp de Havilland Gipsy Queen engine with a constant speed airscrew, they could cruise when new at about 130mph without undue pushing, but old ones flogged to death, left out in all weather literally for years, became very tired and slow. Nevertheless, they stuck it bravely until condemned by their glued joints opening and fungoid growths sprouting amidst the sodden flooring. They performed a yeoman service in training organisations such as ours. True, wings and tails fell off at times with fatal results, but these happenings were rare. It is possible that P6113 had a partial wing failure causing a sudden spin, which could have given little time to react.

His death was reported widely. A book of newspaper cuttings collected by a family friend has tributes from a wide variety of newspapers from all parts of the country. His own local newspaper the *Manchester Evening News* carried this story:

SAGA OF P.T.ECKERSLEY, AIRMAN WHO DID NOT KNOW DEFEAT GROUNDED, FOUGHT BACK TO FLY AGAIN

The Manchester Evening News Air Correspondent, Sept. 13th 1940

Today I am able to reveal the heroic story behind the death on active flying service of Lieut. P.T.Eckersley, M.P. - the sportsman who never knew when he was beaten.

Before the war I often saw him piloting his own plane. He flew into a Manchester aerodrome one night to watch Civil Air Guards training. There was a sparkle in his eyes as he watched a fledging doing a figure of eight and landing in a training machine.

For his heart was in the air. He loved flying just as he loved his cricket. The enthusiasm, the courage, and the devotion he showed when he captained Lancashire went into his flying too.

Back to Politics

And he loved his country. He joined up long before war started. Already a pilot with many hours flying experience he went into training in 1938 to learn to pilot military machines until February 1939. Then he had a bad attack of influenza and bronchitis. He was 'grounded'. Distressed by the doctor's decision he accepted the post of Parliamentary Secretary to Major Gwilym Lloyd George. But this work was not enough. He used to tell his friends: 'I cannot be content with a civilian job that an older man might do.' He insisted he should be allowed to fly again.

So that the doctors would pass him he began to a deliberate plan to get himself fit again. He succeeded, and once more was able to hear the roar of powerful aero engines.

Time after time he went out to fight the enemy. He was happiest in the cockpit.

Then came the fateful day of August 13th. His machine got into a spin. It crashed, caught fire, and Lieut. P.T. Eckersley was killed.

But he died as he would have wished …….in a British fighter defending his country.

His intimate friends will always remember the pride with which he announced the month before he died that he had more flying hours to his credit than any other pilot in his squadron.

Footnote

The bravery and courage of Peter is unquestioned. He had no need to join the Naval Air Reserve; he was turned down once but refused to be beaten and applied again. As a Member of Parliament he was in a reserved occupation but that was never enough for him. He was only happy when he was piloting a plane, rising above his earth-bound existence to experience the freedom and adventure of the air.

Richard Bach, who wrote *Jonathan Livingstone Seagull*, said this in *A Gift of Wings*:

I suspect the thing that makes us fly, whatever it is, is the same thing that draws the sailor out to sea. Some people will never understand why and we can't explain it to them. If they're willing and have an open heart we can show them, but tell them we can't.

It's true. Ask, 'Why fly?' and I should tell you nothing. Instead, I should take you out to the grounds of an airport on a Saturday morning in the end of August. There is sun and cloud in the sky, now, and here's a cool breeze hushing around the precision sculptures of light planes all washed in rainbows and set carefully on the grass. Here's a smell of clean metal and fabric in the air, and the swishing chug of a small engine spinning a little windmill of a propeller making ready to fly. I'm not happy unless there's some air between me and the ground.

I think Peter Eckersley would have understood those sentiments.

7.

Tributes to a gallant man

A GREAT AND SPLENDID ENGLISHMAN

"He was a man of great spiritual confidence; he believed that the sacred cause would prosper and triumph"

Anon

Stained glass window in Chowbent Chapel, Atherton.

LEADERS IN EVERY walk of life mingled together when they stood in the 17th Century Chowbent Unitarian Chapel to pay their respects to Lieut. P.T. Eckersley, M.P., J.P., R.N.V.R. There was a large crowd in the vicinity of the chapel and crowds lined the pavements to Tyldesley Cemetery where the interment took place.

The service was led by Rev. Glyn Evans, a close friend of the family. The hymns *Onward Christian Soldiers* and *The King of Love my Shepherd* were sung. In his address Rev. Evans spoke movingly about Peter:

By his tragic and heroic death Peter Eckersley, a great and splendid Englishman, had ended his earthly course. He had outstanding promise and outstanding personality and the greatest in the land had paid their tributes to him - The Prime Minister, the Speaker of the House of Commons and those who possessed the genius of the game of cricket. The wonderful brother airmen who recognised his kindred spirit. All knew his intrepid courage and consecration to duty. The columns of the National Press had extolled his honour, his name and fame, and they had sent praises to the ends of the earth.

In that House of God, in which his increasing eminence and his developing career had profoundly impressed them, their esteem of him heightened as they witnessed his quiet and unostentatious devotion to religion. Only last Sunday morning he attended service there and had occupied the Eckersley pew near the Eckersley Memorial window with his wife and children. Although he had only 58 hours leave, he had found time to visit the venerable Chowbent Chapel, which he loved so well. Generations of Eckersleys had loved it and served it before him for 300 years. For 15 years Peter had been a Trustee of the chapel like his forbears. One of the profound principles for which Chowbent Chapel had stood throughout the years had been and still was religious liberty. By personal conviction as well as family tradition, Peter Eckersley was a true servant and a soldier of precious human liberty.

In his sublime service to his country and his brave sacrifice for it, are inspiring symbols of the central issue of this war which threatens all human progress and liberty. He knew that his forefathers had dared and served for that deathless cause of liberty and he was equally willing to dare, to suffer, that his liberty might be enjoyed by all upon earth. Here was another memory to treasure. He believed and he had the faith that the sacred cause of liberty would triumph. He believed he had these assurances in his brave heart.

Memorial service at St Ann's Church, Manchester

Hundreds of people, from a ball-boy at Old Trafford to the Lord Lieutenant of Lancashire, attended St. Ann's Church in Manchester for the memorial service to Peter Eckersley. Leaders of political life and of social and educational organisations were there. So were the cricketers he played with and the men he met when he captained Lancashire.

Canon Paton-Williams conducted the service and said Peter Eckersley died as he would wished - playing for England:

We all knew him for that shy reserve which covered a fine sense of solid manhood. Life for him consisted in playing the next stroke, and whether at Old Trafford, at the House of Commons, or in the air he always played the game – a clean game, a good game.

Tributes

From an unnamed M.P.: A Gallant Man:

A few weeks ago during a secret session, I found myself sitting beside Peter Eckersley in the Members' Gallery. I had always liked him for his modesty and his quiet suggestion of character, but we had never exchanged more than a few words at a time. As a former cricket captain of Lancashire he commanded a special respect and when he became Parliamentary Secretary to Major Lloyd George some months ago everyone hoped it might be the beginning of a successful political career.

On the occasion when he sat next to me, he was obviously in a state of excitement that was quite foreign to him. His eyes were sparkling and there was a smile on his slightly flushed cheeks. At last, and rather shyly, he said to me, 'I have had some grand news. I though they wouldn't take me, but I have been passed for flying with the Naval Air Arm.'

I knew he that he had long been a flying enthusiast, but thirty-six seemed rather beyond the age for a fighting pilot. But that was not his idea. With his eyes looking straight into space and with his voice trembling with some inner exultation, he said: 'Isn't it wonderful to get this chance to fight for one's country.'

That was the last time I saw him, and now there has come the news that he has been killed. As I have said, he was quiet undemonstrative, and rather shy, yet I felt then that I had never seen man who loved England more passionately and more nobly. His widow and his two little sons will cherish the simple splendour of his sacrifice long after the wounds of this war have ceased to bleed.

From Capt. Charles Taylor M.P.:

All the time Peter was working in Parliament he was eager to return to active service and he was never happier than on the day he heard back from medical advisors that he could go back to flying. He put on his uniform in the same spirit as he would have prepared for a cricket match, believing that the rest of the side were looking to him for inspiration. At times in his political career the conflict between party ties and conscience was apparent, but his courage and honesty never failed to impress his political opponents. Those who knew him intimately are deeply grieved at losing in the summer of his life the most generous and loyal friend.

From Lord Ebbisham, who organised the Lord's & Commons cricket team:

I first met him at Trent Bridge in 1929 when my county were playing in the County Championship. He came in his own aeroplane, early evidence of his love of flying. When he came to Westminster he was warmly welcomed and became a member of the Lord's and Commons Cricket Club and secretary. We recognized him as a great personality, full of kindness and thought for others and, above all, so modest and unselfish. It is well known that he made his mark in the House. His early death leaves a blank impossible to fill. His countless friends, both on and off the field, will ever revere his memory.

From Sir Patrick Hannon M.P.:

The sad news of the death of Peter Eckersley on active service has been received by his colleagues in the House of Commons with deep sorrow and regret. He was one of the most vigorous, attractive and forceful younger members of the House. His personal charm, virile character and abounding energy won the admiration and esteem of all who came in contact with him. His work on the Air Committee was persistent, constructive and inspiring. He came from that wholesome and sturdy Lancashire stock which has down the ages made a contribution of abiding uplift to the march of British directive power in world affairs.

When he entered the House he became almost at once an intimate friend of older members like myself, who could recall the great social and political services of his family to the public life of this great country. While he was still a child many of us who were active in the tariff battles of 30 years ago were the guests of his father and mother at their charming home at Newton-le-Willows. He was in the supreme sense of the word a sportsman and a gentleman. His memory will remain green and revered among a host of friends in and out of Parliament who will always be proud of the friendship and stimulating qualities of a gallant gentleman who not merely advocated the expansion of air power but has made the supreme sacrifice that British civilisation might survive.

From Lancashire wicket-keeper George Duckworth:

Peter's friends talked about him today, a thing he would never do about himself. Peter was a Peter Pan in his way, for he never seemed to grow up. He was a charming personality, so boyish and full of fun. He loved a joke – even against himself – and when he was captain of the side there were many comedians in it, and we used to have grand times. On tour he would come round at night to see we were all comfortable. When he was an M.P. he always looked forward to the Lancashire team visiting the south. He took them round the Houses of Parliament, introduced them to many northern M.P.s and gave them dinner in the House. His death is a great loss to cricket, as he was destined to become the head of Lancashire County Cricket Club at a future time. I am very distressed at his passing.

From Mr. T.A. Higson, Lancashire chairman and family friend:

I have known Peter since he was seven. He was one of the few people I have known who worthily fulfilled every duty and obligation. He brought Lancashire cricket to a very high standard, and he was loved by all his sporting colleagues. As an M.P. he did very well in such a short time. He had the welfare of his constituents at heart.

When he could spare the time he played a very good game of tennis. He was very modest, and not at all the kind of flamboyant personality about whom stories are always being told. He was kind beyond description and could never do enough for his many friends. No-one appealed to him for help in vain.

From Cec Parkin, Lancashire cricketer and friend:

Peter came to see me some little time ago. He was yearning to be back with the Fleet Air Arm where his flying experience could be of service to his country. It was typical of Peter. I knew him from his boyhood. I coached him in Leigh and he might have been a really great cricketer. But he mixed his cricket with flying and his flying with politics to the neglect of his cricket. He was a charming fellow, a wonderful personality.

And a final tribute be from Major Rupert Howard, secretary of Lancashire C.C.C.:

He was one of the younger members of the club to whom the control and future of Lancashire cricket would obviously have been entrusted. And it would have been in safe and capable hands.

Peter died at the age of only 36. What he could have achieved in a long parliamentary career and also in the future of Lancashire cricket, one could only speculate. But like so many young men who sacrificed their lives for their country in war we will never know.

As well as the memorial at Old Trafford there are memorials at Rugby School and also Trinity College Cambridge. Peter was associated with Bowdon Cricket Club and his name appears on their war memorial. There is also the window and memorial to Peter at his church, Chowbent Unitarian Chapel as well as in the House of Commons.

Peter Eckersley's memorial at Westminster.

8.

Not forgotten

"Let us remember before God, and commend to his sure keeping, those who have died for their country in war and peace; those whom we knew, and those whose memory we treasure, and all who lived and died in the service of their country and mankind."

ON TUESDAY 6TH September 2022, the second day of the Roses match against Yorkshire at Old Trafford a small ceremony was held to honour the only Lancashire player killed in the Second World War. The plaque was unveiled by his grandson William Eckersley and present were the family of Sidney Snow, the young air-gunner killed with Peter in the crash.

We were hoping that the Bentley which Peter owned in 1928 and has now been restored would be able to be there but it was not possible. Martin Crocker has written about that Bentley in the appendix.

Peter died as he would have wished, in a British aeroplane defending his country. At the time of his death he had more flying hours to his credit than any other pilot in his squadron.

I felt privileged to lead the small service and to remember Lancashire's most charismatic player and also one of the bravest.

I found Peter's life to be very interesting and lived at a very fast pace. Perhaps he was never meant to make old bones. Living life on the fast lane with his high performance Bentley, the dangerous sports, usually abroad and involving all kinds of risks on the ice and snow. Taking up flying when it was still in its early days and dangerous. Not only buying his own aircraft but finding a wife who shared his enthusiasms and was an accomplished pilot in her own right.

His life and career seemed to be lived at a fast pace with many changes of direction. Not for Peter merely following his father into the family firms, although he had directorships but didn't seem to have the time to develop them. There was always an urgency about him. He took his risk-taking and some could say a cavalier attitude into the game of cricket and his captaincy. Captaining Lancashire to two championship titles was never going to be enough, and he retired at an age when he could easily have gone on for a few more years. But serving his country in Parliament was always there, and two unsuccessful attempts at election did not thwart him, it just steeled his determination.

I think Parliament was the field where he found he could express himself and also serve his constituents. When the impending war arrived there was no question that he wouldn't offer himself for service. At thirty-six he was old for a fighter pilot and the medical people had their doubts, but again, Peter would not be defeated despite his role as a Member of Parliament which exempted himself for military service. Although it was a reserved occupation he wanted to serve his country and wouldn't take no for an answer.

Whilst researching and writing this booklet I felt I have got to know and like Peter Eckersley. He is forgotten no longer. Peter wasn't among the greatest of Lancashire cricketers with bat and ball but no other player can match his qualities of Charisma, Loyalty, Leadership, Bravery, Courage and Sacrifice.

I would have liked to have met Peter Eckersley (he would be carrying his rolled umbrella) and shake him by the hand. His story had been forgotten but I am pleased I have brought it to life with the help of his grandson William.

I do hope I have done Peter Eckersley justice in this booklet for his story greatly moved me. I hope it has done the same for you.

Rev. Malcolm G. Lorimer
Heritage Team, Lancashire C.C.C.

Peter Eckersley's memorial in the House of Commons chamber.

Appendices

1. Peter Eckersley - first class career record — 115

2. Peter Eckersley - family and descendants — 117

3. India - letters to Lord's about the tour — 119

4. Worthy Down - crash site — 131

5. Peter Eckersley - war record — 133

6. Sidney John Snow - naval airman — 135

7. Percival Proctor - airplane — 137

8. Bentley - RA4578 — 139

1.

Peter Eckersley - first class career record

SEASON BY SEASON RECORD

Season	M	Inns	NO	Runs	HS	Ave	100	50	Ct
1923 (England)	1	1	0	0	0	0.00	0	0	0
1924 (England)	2	4	1	47	32*	15.66	0	0	2
1925 (England)	10	12	1	222	82*	20.18	0	1	3
1926 (England)	14	19	2	355	99	20.88	0	2	5
1926/27 (Sri Lanka)	4	5	2	89	39*	29.66	0	0	2
1926/27 (India)	22	27	3	702	86	29.25	0	3	3
1927 (England)	26	26	3	636	102*	27.65	1	2	15
1927/28 (West Indies)	1	2	0	52	50	26.00	0	1	0
1929 (England)	31	36	6	440	78*	14.66	0	2	10
1929/30 (Argentina)	3	5	0	134	88	26.80	0	1	1
1930 (England)	32	40	11	855	86	29.48	0	5	31
1931 (England)	29	35	4	389	50	12.54	0	1	12
1932 (England)	25	28	4	277	44	11.54	0	0	17
1933 (England)	31	32	4	620	85*	22.14	0	5	19
1934 (England)	29	32	5	485	91	17.96	0	2	8
1935 (England)	30	32	5	324	36*	12.00	0	0	13
1936 (England)	1	1	0	0	0	0.00	0	0	0
1938 (England)	1	2	0	2	2	1.00	0	0	0

TEAM BY TEAM RECORD

Team	M	Inns	NO	Runs	HS	Ave	100	50	Ct
England XI	1	2	0	2	2	1.00	0	0	0
Gentlemen	1	1	0	36	36	36.00	0	0	0
Lancashire	256	293	45	4588	102*	18.50	1	20	133
LH Tennyson's XI	1	2	0	52	50	26.00	0	1	0
MCC	30	36	6	817	86	27.23	0	3	7
Sir J Cahn's XI	3	5	0	134	88	26.80	0	1	1

Above: with sons Peter and Roger and the pet dog.
Below: The family's new home at Midways in Ashley.

2.

Peter Eckersley - family and descendants

PETER ECKERSLEY'S SONS were Peter (b. 1933) and Roger (b. 1935). They were both born in Manchester and raised in the family home in Ashley. After their father's death, and like many others at the time, there was no time or space for grief. Soon they were at boarding school, where their love of cricket flourished (and all other sports.) Later both worked in different parts of the insurance industry, with Peter having three children quite early in life: David, Clare and Suzie, while Roger was late in having William, Fergus and Olivia. The brothers remained great friends throughout until Peter's early death in his late 50s.

Audrey eventually moved away from Lancashire to Buckinghamshire where she married Sam Crichton-Maitland. They met and married sometime after the war. Sam's daughters, Judith and Sally, became half-sisters to Roger and Peter and remained close throughout their lives. Sam had been an army Lt-Col during the war and later worked in the motor trade, running a Jaguar dealership near their home around Sevenoaks. He died in the early 1970s.

Audrey then married Maurice Allom, the former England and Kent Cricketer. Maurice had been a friend of the Eckersleys for many years and had been on cricket tours with Peter. He is one of only three players to have taken a hat-trick on Test debut in what was New Zealand's first ever Test match. In the same Test he also became the first Test player to take four wickets in five balls.

He served as Surrey's President from 1970 to 1977, and as President of Marylebone Cricket Club in 1969–70. He was amember of M.C.C. for 70 years, from 1925 until his death. He was also a skilful saxophonist, who played in Fred Elizalde's band in the 1920s.

Allom had been married for almost half a century to Pamela, who died in 1980. It was after Pamela died that he married Audrey. His son Anthony played first-class cricket for Surrey and was one of the tallest people to have played the game, standing between 6 ft 9 ins and 6 ft 10 ins.

Audrey died in 1994 aged 90.

With Best Wishes

from

The Madras Cricket Club

3.

India - letters to Lord's about the tour

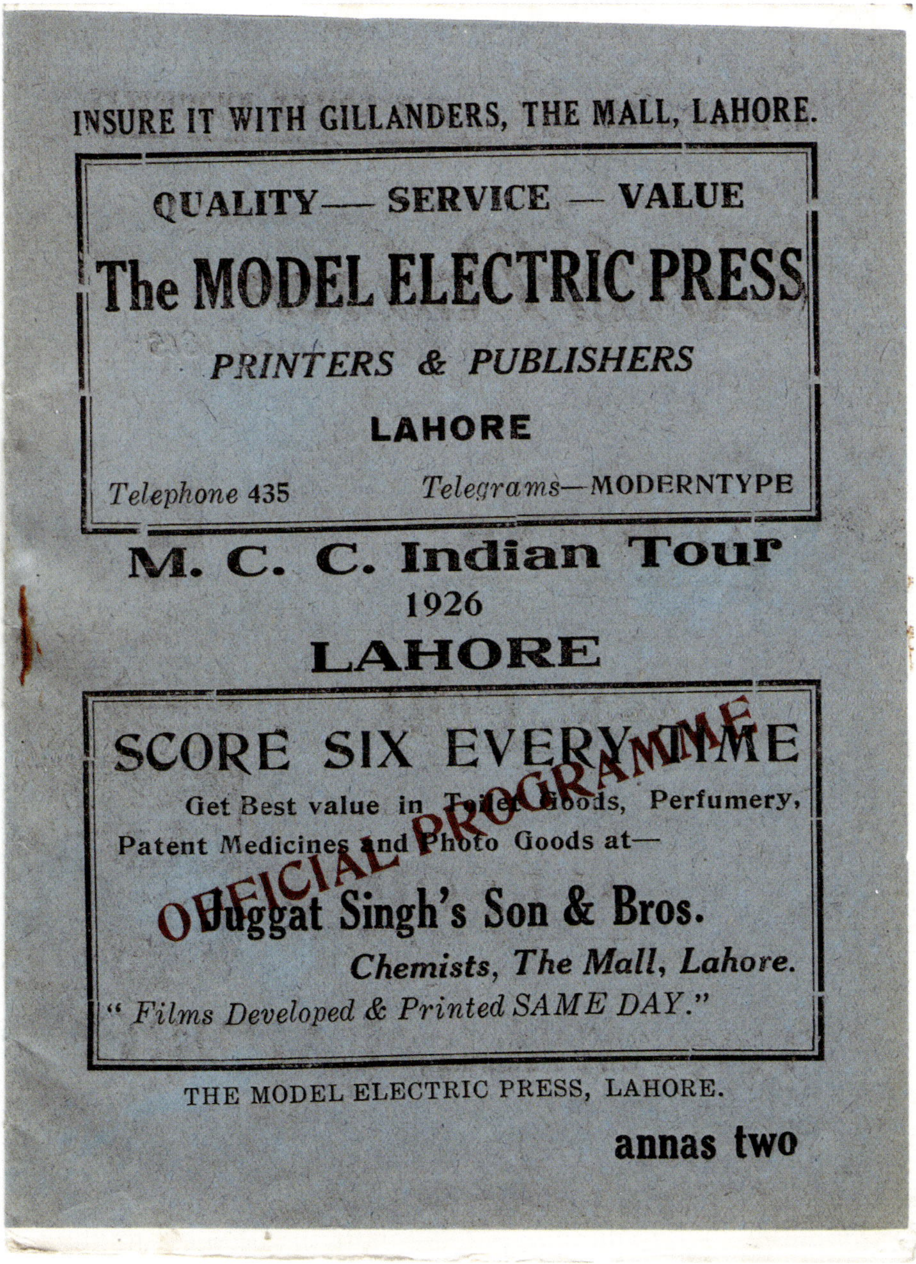

INSURE IT WITH GILLANDERS, THE MALL, LAHORE.

QUALITY — SERVICE — VALUE

The MODEL ELECTRIC PRESS

PRINTERS & PUBLISHERS

LAHORE

Telephone 435　　　Telegrams—MODERNTYPE

M. C. C. Indian Tour
1926
LAHORE

SCORE SIX EVERY TIME
Get Best value in Toilet Goods, Perfumery, Patent Medicines and Photo Goods at—
Juggat Singh's Son & Bros.
Chemists, The Mall, Lahore.
"Films Developed & Printed SAME DAY."

OFICIAL PROGRAMME

THE MODEL ELECTRIC PRESS, LAHORE.

annas two

Lord's Cricket Ground,
London, N.W.8

Copy.

Carlton Club,
Pall Mall, S.W.1.
21st August, 1926.

Dear Sir,

Sir Francis Lacey will be writing you officially on the subject of the approaching tour; but I feel that I may - having interested myself in the matter, and been perhaps instrumental in persuading the M.C.C. Committee to risk sending a mixed team to India, and to shoulder the extremely heavy financial burden involved - address you in the friendly spirit of a cricketer; and I should be glad if you would cause the gist of these remarks to be conveyed confidentially to the chief centres of cricket activities in India. They are not for the Press.

We have received several friendly warnings to send a much larger number than 13: but that is impossible partly because it only leads to dissatisfaction if several members who have undertaken the tour in order to play cricket have to stand out of a good many matches because there are no casualties amongst the eleven best: and secondly because this team is quite expensive enough. Players' fees and amateurs' pocket money, though considerably less than what is given for Australian tours, which correspond as regards length of absence, will absorb nearly the whole of the Rs. 40,000 you have guaranteed, leaving practically nothing for travelling to, from and in India, unless the Rupee is worth a good deal better than 1s: and even then the excess over your guarantee must be so great as to fully justify our having pressed you for the most liberal possible concession out of your profits if such accrue.

You might be disposed to criticise us for sending so expensive a team: if so we must ask you to remember that you told us it was no use to send a team unless there were attractive individuals in it.

It has been impossible to get the leading amateurs: Gentlemen cannot afford an absence of six months from the

(2)

University, the Professions or from business, and we deem ourselves particularly fortunate to have secured as many first class players as we have done. We had no option, therefore, if we were to send a team qualified to maintain the prestige of English cricket, but to fill up with first class professionals. There is a great demand for these men - such as have not established businesses - for winter work all the world over, and the remuneration they can get for such engagements is a factor in determining the fees we give.

To comply with your wish for Star performers we asked Hobbs, Sutcliffe, Hendren, Woolley, Kilner; but none, though all would have liked to go, could manage it. We are sending you nevertheless an extremely fine team, all, but perhaps one, fit to play in Gentlemen v Players and many have actually done so.

Mr. Gilligan is a captain of great experience and a brilliant player; but to enable him to put the best energies into the matches it is essential he should not be troubled with the detail of travelling. We wish we could have sent a manager but the additional expense is a deterrent. I have taken the liberty of warning your representatives at home, and beg to repeat to you that we trust you will find some benevolent person at each match centre who will look after details and save Gilligan from petty worries, and will hand him over to someone else at the next centre.

There is another somewhat important matter - viz., as regards entertainments of a public character, outside of Government Houses. We must ask you to realise that on these tours there is no distinction of social rank: all are equal in the Republic of Cricket, and if invitations of a public character were made they must include the players as well as the amateurs. As regards Government House entertainment, if any such are offered, I have submitted for H.E. the Viceroy's consideration a practically similar suggestion.

I understand there is some idea of Mrs. Earle accompanying her husband, if so he will have to make his own arrangements for her comfort.

I hope you will find the team individually pleasant guests; we have taken great trouble to secure this, and it only remains for me on behalf of the Committee of M.C.C. to commend them to your kind consideration,

Believe me,
Yours faithfully,
(signed) HARRIS.

No. 1.

Copy.
From the Honorary Secretary,
Calcutta Cricket Club.

105 Clive Street,
Calcutta,
29th March, 1927.

My dear Findlay,

It is with some reluctance that I set about this letter to you, but things have got to such a pass that neither my Committee nor I feel inclined to sit down under these constant attacks directed against our courtesy and our arrangements.

In the report that appeared in the "Statesman" of March 28th, it is alleged that that Gilligan said that certain Clubs were guilty of snobbishness, and the report of the remarks which he made just before embarking for England contained the following:-

"He went on to say that he had one grievance regarding the tour that it had been badly arranged there being too much unnecessary travelling especially towards the end of it. We are after all only human. The trains we travelled in were disgraceful at times it seems we were given the worse carriages on the line. They were hardly fit for sheep to travel in and sometimes were not swept out for days. This however, is the only grouse I have".

I now give an extract from Lucas' letter of the 26th March - Lucas is the Honorary Secretary of the Bombay Gymkhana, and, incidently, an officer of the Bombay, Baroda and Central India Railway.

"He (referring to Gilligan) made some very ungracious remarks about Indian railways. In our case, travelling from Delhi to Ajmere they had the use of 2 Bends of Departments, saloons (large ones - new ones). Coming from Viramgam the other day I arranged for them to have a corridor (first with Restaurant Car connected so as to avoid their having to get out of their carriage for a meal, and that was on a train that does not run a Restaurant car and leaves Ahmedabad at 9.30 p.m. and gets in here at 8.40 a.m. They could not have been done better.

Now, as far as the East Indian Railway is concerned I happen to be the Secretary to the Agent of the E.I.Railway (Agent being General Manager)

We put on a first class bogie coach - an entirely new one - at their disposal. This coach was attached to the Punjab Mail (which is the most important train in India) as far as Tundla, which is the junction for Agra. This coach was detached at Tundla and put on the branch line for Agra so that the team should not have to change. They stopped at Agra for nearly 24 hours and the coach was kept waiting for them.

It was then attached to their train taking them to Aligarh, where it was again kept waiting for them for the two days they were there. It was then attached to their train for Delhi

No. 2 continued.

where it was finally released. All this was done without charging for demurrage or hire charges which is the usual railway practice. All railways in India gave them first class accomodation for 2nd class fares and half 1st class tickets for their servants. Apart from this we put a railway clerk at their disposal the whole way up to Delhi to look after their luggage without charging anything. If any two railways could have done more than the B.B. and C.I. and the E.I.Rlwys, I shall be mighty surprised, and I feel sure that West, who is an officer of the North Western Railway, and honorary Secretary at Lahore looked after them equally well.

The carriage which brought them into Calcutta from Bombay was an old one, and, of course, travelling across India is dirty work - you cannot keep out of the dust - There are, however, always sweepers at big stations to clean the compartments and they are generally only too anxious to do their work for the sake of a small tip. I really think that Gilligan should be told to withdraw his remarks which are, I consider, entirely devoid of truth. They will cost the next tour a good Rs10,000/-.

Now about the itinerary - you know that I explained that they had to go all the way to Colombo and back because of the climatic conditions. I told Gilligan this in Calcutta, and he begged me to arrange for a boat to bring them back to Calcutta this we did, and really the last portion of their travelling was not very arduous. They went to Rangoon by boat, from Rangoon to Madras by boat, from Madras to Colombo by rail and from Colombo to Calcutta by boat; so from the north to the south of India and back they only did about 400 miles by rail, and their journey from Calcutta to Agra, Delhi and Patiala was very much broken up.

Gilligan wrote to me on March 15th complaining about his journey from Viramgam to Bombay (this journey is dealt with in the latter half of the extract from Lucas' letter quoted above) I personally explained to him when he was in Calcutta that I felt somewhat anxious about their travelling after they had left Delhi, because the matter had been entirely taken out of my hands.

You see, Patiala promised to look after them up to his place and Ranji had undertaken, I understood, to look after them from Patiala to Jammanagar and on to Bombay; in fact, I was under the impression from what Gilligan said that they were going by boat from Ranji's place to Bombay in order to catch the mail. It was entirely impossible for me to make arrangements as you will see I did not even know they were travelling by train. If he had wired me a day or two before I might possibly have fixed up with the B.B. & C.I.Railway for their fares to be paid. We have, of course paid them, but the reason why Bombay did not pay them was that all their M.C.C. accounts had been closed and Lucas explained that to them I understand.

I am certain that there was not a single hitch in the travelling arrangements which the various centres or myself made.

No 3 continued.

Now about "snobbishness" of clubs in Calcutta, the whole team were made Honorary Members of the U.S. Club, Royal Calcutta Golf Club, Calcutta Cricket Club; they were all given complimentary tickets to the Turf Club, which admitted them to the Members' enclosure and stand. I think I am right in saying, although I am open to correction, that not a single member of the team put their foot inside either the U.S. or the Royal.

The Calcutta Cricket Club cannot dictate to the Bengal Clubs or to the Saturday Club, neither of which made the Pros. Honorary Members, but the Amateurs used the Saturday Club frequently, and most of the Pros. were brought in by members. Gilligan told Toby Campbell that the whole team were very dissatisfied with the way they had been treated in Calcutta, and they feel all this very keenly. Gilligan has left out any reference to Calcutta and Bombay when he has spoken about the places they have visited, and if any Committee worked to give them as far as possible my Committee did.

Since I started this letter I have received one from Hill which I enclose in original. As late as though fit to write so, I will tell you what happened which I would not otherwise have done. I have told you that the team came from Colombo to Calcutta by boat. There had been a shipping strike in Colombo, and a report in the papers had stated that their boat was delayed, anyhow we did not expect her in till the morning of February 15th, on the evening of which date they were due to start for Agra and Aligarh. I had, therefore, made no arrangements for the night of the 14th - 15th. It was not till the morning of the 14th that I knew their boat was coming in that afternoon and immediately after breakfast I went round to the Grand Hotel and reserved 14 rooms for them which I got at a concession rate as I told the Manager it was a good advertisement for them to have the M.C.C. there.

I could'nt go down to the boat to meet them myself because I was very busy in office, and I had already taken a fortnight's leave to look after them when they were playing here. But Rosie, Campbell and Garnett all went, and I sent a note to Gilligan explaining what I had arranged. A Railway lorry met them for their luggage and a Cooks' man was engaged to help them through the Customs.

When they got to the Hotel the man in charge of the booking office told them they could only have six rooms, but when my letter to Gilligan was shown to him he gave them 13 rooms as two of the team had accepted invitations to stay with friends in Calcutta, although they had not let me know this. I went to the Hotel immediately after office and asked them if they would like any of us to dine with them and they said "Oh no" we shall all be out" or something like that. The following evening I went

No 4. continued.

round again and found a difficulty about their drink bills, as the management did not want to free their luggage without payment, so I at once signed an undertaking that the Calcutta Cricket Club would pay for all their drinks as well as their ordinary Hotel expenses (query - is it the custom for touring sides to have all their drinks paid, for Gilligan insisted on this?) Now about the dispatch case - When we were seeing them off at the station, Hill dashed up and said the Hotel had refused to give him/however his dispatch case because he said he had thrown a pillow which pricked him on the floor.

We made immediate enquiries and found that what had occurred was this. Hill had taken his pillow, ripped off the pillow case and torn it in half - he had also torn the pillow almost in half. Campbell saw it. But apart from this in one of the other rooms the basin and lead piping had been ripped away from the wall and we had to pay a bill' for Rs 75/ That is why the dispatch case was detained. We, of course, got hold of it at once and sent it at/might to Aligarh as Hill was not long without it. I hold no brief for the Grand Hotel - there is not a comfortable Hotel in Calcutta, but there is no excuse for such behaviour, and I object to the tone of Hill's letter, though I much regret that his things should have been broken.

As I have said before, I am sorry to have to write this to you, but feel there is no other course open to me in view of what has occurred.

With kindest regards,

Yours sincerely,

(signed) M.Robertson.

GOVERNMENT HOUSE
MAHABLESHWAR

19th April 1927.

My dear Harris,

Many thanks for your letter of the 22nd March, with the enclosure from the M.C.C. Committee. I hope you will tell the Committee that I am very grateful for their recognition of any small thing I could do for the M.C.C. team, and that any such help was given with the greatest possible pleasure.

Jacker stayed with me for a couple of days on his way to Calcutta, and I think he found those two days very useful, as he and Lady Jackson, and all the members of their staff, spent the whole 48 hours in trying to pick up any useful tips about Government Houses; while he and I had many long talks on the situation out here. He went off in a spirit of much optimism, but with the realisation – which I think he had gained in England, and had not lost out here – that Bengal was not the easiest of the Provinces in India to deal with politically. I have heard from him twice and he writes fairly cheerfully, although complaining somewhat of the heat at Calcutta; but he has now got off to Darjeeling.

You ask me in your letter to let you have, confidentially, any gup from Calcutta about the behaviour of Gilligan's team. There has been a great deal of comment in the Calcutta Press and by individuals on Gilligan's accusation of snobbishness, which, of course, was directed against Calcutta. I know a good deal about it, and, as for myself, I am convinced that the whole fault lay, in the first instance, with the Europeans in Calcutta. If they

had....

2.

had only adopted the policy we adopted in Bombay with regard to the Clubs, I do not think that any feeling would have arisen. I knew myself that the question of professionals and amateurs would be difficult in Bombay, as there were certain Clubs here (the Byculla and the Yacht Club for instance) which could not, under their rules, ask the professionals to become honorary members; and I told them that, if this were the case and they could not make an exception, it was far preferable that they should issue no invitation to the M.C.C. at all. They agreed, and I explained the whole position to Gilligan, who fully agreed also. In Calcutta, however, two of the principal Clubs sent invitations to the amateurs only, and the professionals were extremely annoyed, and Gilligan had a very hard task in calming them down – which, however, he did successfully. Then, also, it was unfortunate that the M.C.C. team were at Calcutta at Christmas, when the whole of Calcutta is so occupied with its Xmas entertaining, races, etc. As you know, Xmas Week in Calcutta is an occasion for entertainments which have been the custom for years, and not even the advent of the M.C.C. team could upset those time-honoured gaieties.

Frankly, for anything that occurred, I do not think Gilligan is to blame at all, and it is unfortunate that the control of cricket in India should be in the hands (as it was for this tour) of the Calcutta Cricket Club, which is composed entirely of Europeans, and not in any way representative of Indian cricket. I am not saying this because I am in Bombay and have any feelings such as we are supposed to have against Calcutta; but I am endeavouring, now, – not with much success at the moment – to get Europeans and Indians to organise an Indian Cricket Control Board, which will be representative of all cricket in India, and which will be responsible for any future tours of visiting cricketers, or for any teams we may send from India to tour. I

have....

3.

have to walk very carefully in this, and I am refusing to let my own name appear at present, as I know that I should be accused by Calcutta of wanting to take, for Bombay, the control of cricket in India; and the first steps which are being taken are through the Quadrangular Cricket Committee – which is, as a matter of fact, in Bombay, but which is the only real representative body of European and Indian cricket combined.

It is, of course, extremely easy to find fault with some actions of a team of 15 men playing cricket continuously for many months in a country like India, where they have to put up with considerable inconvenience, and where their health naturally suffered at times from the climate; but I myself am quite convinced that Gilligan deserves every praise for the tactful manner in which he ran the tour, and that he and all his men, amateurs and professionals, played the game in every way, both on the field and off. Gilligan had no easy task, and the result of the tour, both as regards the cricket and everything else, reflected much credit on him. He was most ably assisted, as he would be the first to admit, by Chichester-Constable.

I am afraid I have been a bit lengthy, but I knew you wanted to hear my honest and full opinion.

Yours sincerely,

Leslie Wilson.

The Right Hon'ble Lord Harris,
    GCSI., GCIE., CB.
    8. Old Jewry.

4.

Worthy Down - crash site

ON 24 MAY, 1939 Worthy Down was officially handed over to the Admiralty and named HMS Kestrel. The field became home to the 1 Telegraphist Air Gunners School (TAG). No 1 Air Gunners School came shortly afterwards with three flying units, Nos 755, 756 and 757, equipped with Blackburn Shark and Hawker Ospreys. For a brief period between 29 June 1939 and 29 July of the same year 814 Squadron, a Torpedo Spotter Reconnaissance unit, brought their Fairey Swordfish in before deploying to HMS Ark Royal.

Hitler, at this time, continued to see how far he could pursue his goals, and up until now, he had suffered little in the way of consequences for his aggression. However, his invasion of Poland on 1 September 1939 was a step too far and resulted in Britain and France declaring war on Germany on 3 September 1939.

The TAG School was still resident when war broke out and was joined at the airfield by the survivors of 811 and 822 Squadron following the sinking of the carrier HMS Courageous (torpedoed by U-29 on 17 September 1939). The two units amalgamated to become 815 Squadron (Swordfish I) before disbanding again in November 1939 and merging with 774 Squadron. Between 10 to 16 November 1939, 774 Squadron formed at the site as an Armament Training Squadron for observers, with a selection of Sharks, Skuas, Rocs and Swordfish. The unit was equipped by taking aircraft and personnel from 782 and 815 Squadrons and storage. To say their stay was brief would be an understatement, as they had left for Aldergrove within six days.

On 1 February 1940, 806 Squadron formed at Worthy Down as a fighter unit equipped with four Blackburn Skuas and four Rocs. The squadron moved to Hatston on 28 March of the same year and undertook bombing operations against oil targets at Bergen during the Norwegian Campaign. Following the German invasion of Norway on 9 April 1940, the carrier HMS Glorious was ordered back to Britain from Alexandria. One of the ship's squadrons, 825, disembarked and flew to Worthy Down on 4 May 1940.

Since the war began on 3 September 1939, there had been little in the way of action on the Continent. However, this all changed on 10 May 1940 when Hitler launched his Blitzkrieg against the Low Countries and France, catching the Allies completely off guard. The TAG School, which had moved to Jersey on 11 March, swiftly returned to Worthy Down as the Germans overran France.

The British and French armies were pushed back towards the Channel coast, which led to the evacuation at Dunkirk. After returning from Hatston on 26 May 1940, 806 Squadron deployed the following day from Worthy Down to RNAS Detling to lend their assistance in covering the withdrawal from the beaches.

Also deploying to Detling were 825 Squadron, commanded by Lt Cdr Eugene Esmonde. The situation was desperate, which led to the unit's Swordfish undertaking operations outside of their usual remit. By the end of May and June, it was carrying out bombing raids against gun batteries, tanks and transport in the Calais area and spotting for the guns of HMS Arethusa. In such a hostile environment, 825 lost eight aircraft and were withdrawn back to Worthy Down in early July 1940, leaving on 5 September to embark on HMS Furious. Esmonde was later to win a DSO for a torpedo attack on the 52,000-ton German battleship, Bismarck, on 24 May 1941, which he led with eight Swordfish of 825 NAS flying from HMS Victorious.

During this attack, the squadron scored one confirmed hit on the ship when a torpedo struck the armoured belt just below the waterline. However, the damage was minimal, and it fell to 818 NAS flying from HMS Ark Royal to land a mortal blow the following day when a torpedo struck the ship's rudder, jamming it in a 15-degree turn to port. Unable to manoeuver, Bismark was sunk on 27 May 1941 by a Royal Navy task force. Esmonde would go on to win a posthumous Victoria Cross for his heroic leadership during the Channel Dash on 12 February 1942.

Returning to their home airfield, 806's pilots collected the first Fairey Fulmar aircraft to enter service and left for Eastleigh to undergo further training. The Rolls-Royce Merlin-powered Fulmar was designed as a carrier-borne fighter/reconnaissance aircraft crewed by a pilot and observer.

After the Fall of France in June 1940, there was a brief respite of around six weeks before the Battle of Britain began. On 1 July 1940, 808 Squadron formed at the airfield equipping with Fulmar Is. They were present during the Battle of Britain but were not called upon to participate in the fight with the Luftwaffe in southern skies. The unit moved to Castletown on 5 September 1940 to protect Royal Navy assets at Scapa Flow from potential aerial attack.

As the threat of attacks on airfields from the Luftwaffe escalated, decoys were constructed to draw the attention of enemy aircraft to sites where the dropping of bombs would cause little in the way of material damage. Worthy Down's Q/QF decoy site was constructed approximately three miles northeast on open land near the village of Micheldever.

With his victory in France complete, Hitler was convinced the British would see the hopelessness of their position and would come to terms. Churchill was having none of it and vowed to fight on. The Battle of Britain began on 10 July 1940, and, at this time, Luftwaffe attacks were mainly targeted against shipping in the English Channel and ports with some inland bombing raids. The objectives for these attacks had been set out in Hitler Directives No 9, Instructions for Warfare Against the Economy of the Enemy, and No 13, issued on 29 November 1939 and 24 May 1940, respectively. The first of these Directives detailed the most effective means to ensure the crippling of the English economy, and the second authorised attacks against the British homeland, shipping and a host of other assets, as referenced in Directive No 9.

The attacks aimed to deprive Britain of the means to fight by stopping imports for the war effort and denying access to the waters. It also attempted to bring the RAF into the skies to weaken it through attrition. The results were slow in coming when it was considered the number of vessels using the Channel. Although there were losses to the Luftwaffe attacks, Britain showed no signs of capitulating, so this could be seen as a failure to achieve the objective of pacifying the nation by denying it supplies. Hitler was growing impatient with the stubborn British and concluded invasion may be necessary. To this end, on 16 July 1940, he issued Directive No 16, On Preparations for a Landing Operation Against England. He states:

Since England, in spite of her hopeless military situation, shows no signs of being ready to come to an understanding, I have decided to prepare a landing operation against England and, if necessary, to carry it out.

On 1 August, he issued Directive No 17, For The Conduct of Air and Sea Warfare Against England:

In order to establish the necessary conditions for the final conquest of England, I intend to intensify air and sea warfare against the English homeland.

This Directive called for the Luftwaffe to gain air superiority over the Channel and mainland to allow an unhindered invasion to proceed. Part of the plan was to attack airfields, which commenced on 13 August 1940 and was given the name Adlertag (Eagle Day). Although Hermann Göring, head of the Luftwaffe, was confident his air force could sweep the RAF's fighters from the skies, history in time would prove him wrong.

Aerial photo of Worthy Down.

On 15 August 1940, Worthy Down found itself a target of Directive No 17 when the Luftwaffe sent Junkers Ju88A-1s of I/LG1 and II/LG1 from Orleans-Bricy to attack targets in the south of England. The raid was escorted by Messerschmitt Bf 110s of II/ZG76. Despite the constant attention of Hurricanes and Spitfires from 43, 249, 601 and 609 Squadrons over Southampton and the Solent, the raiders eventually got through. In the early evening, the airfield was dive-bombed by II/LG1, causing little in the way of damage. An eyewitness account states a few broken windows, lights and a car windscreen. However, the cost to the Luftwaffe was high, including the loss of five Ju88s to 601 Squadron. The site defences also put up a good show, with a Lewis gun party on a hangar claiming hits on the bombers. Interestingly a gun turret from a Blackburn Roc had been pressed into service and claimed strikes, as did Maxim gun crews.

Middle Wallop was also bombed with minimal effect; the Luftwaffe would have done better to concentrate their efforts on this airfield as it was a critical Fighter Command Sector Station. Worthy Down was, however, not a fighter station, so it's unclear why it was targeted. German intelligence was clearly lacking, and a number of airfields were attacked where the effect of lessening fighter strength was not going to be achieved. The Luftwaffe had planned that Worthy Down was to be targeted on Eagle Day itself by II/LG1, but poor weather and fighter opposition saved it this day.

The 15 August was a bad day for the Luftwaffe and was known to the crews as Black Thursday. On this day, the RAF lost 34 fighters, but for the Germans 75 aircraft did not return from the over 2,000 sorties flown. At a later date, Lord Haw-Haw was to make one of his more notorious remarks when he informed the British public that HMS Kestrel had been

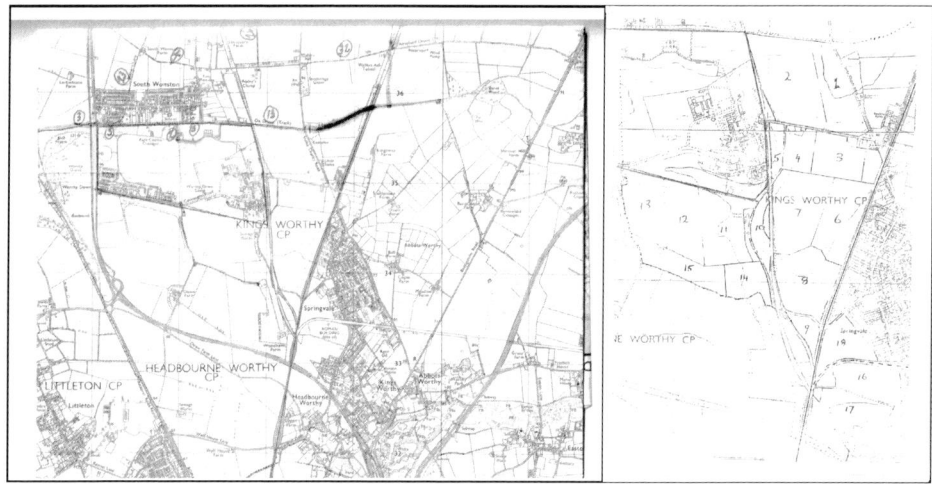

Maps of Worthy Down.

bombed and sunk. This undoubtedly caused some amusement to the station personnel, whose feet were obviously still dry.

While Worthy Down had been lucky to escape damage, the Supermarine Factory at Woolston was less so. On Tuesday, 24 September 1940, the Luftwaffe attacked the complex, killing or injuring many workers but not putting the plant out of action. Two days later, the Luftwaffe struck again and caused more serious damage to Spitfire manufacturing.

Following this, urgent dispersal of Spitfire production became a priority and arrangements were hastily implemented. It was fortunate that the machinery and jigs at Woolston were not destroyed by the bombing. This enabled the equipment to be moved to allow dispersed production. The ingenuity shown was incredible as all manner of premises were commandeered to produce the many thousands of components that make up a Spitfire.

Two Bellman Hangars became available at Worthy Down, and in December 1940, Spitfire development flying was moved to the airfield with Jeffrey Quill, chief test pilot for Vickers-Armstrong, placed in charge. In addition, Spitfires from dispersed sites such as Chattis Hill were flown into Worthy Down for flight testing and onward transit to frontline squadrons.

5.

Peter Eckersley - war record

Record Details for Peter Thorp Eckersley (Royal Naval Volunteer Reserve)

← Back   🖶 Print This Page

☆ Save this Record   ≡ View All Saved Records   ⮘ Share This Record

First Name:	Peter Thorp
Initials:	P T
Surname:	Eckersley
DOB:	Circa 1904
Age:	36
Nationality:	British
Date of Death:	13/08/1940
Information:	SON OF WILLIAM ECKERSLEY, C.B.E., J.P., AND EVA MARY ECKERSLEY (NEE THORP), OF TYLDESLEY; HUSBAND OF AUDREY E. J. ECKERSLEY, OF ASHLEY, CHESHIRE. J.P., MEMBER OF PARLIAMENT FOR EXCHANGE DIVISION OF MANCHESTER, 1935-40; CAPTAIN LANCASHIRE COUNTY CRICKET CLUB, 1929-35.
Rank:	Lieutenant
Service:	Royal Naval Volunteer Reserve
Regiment:	Royal Naval Volunteer Reserve
Battalion:	H.M.S. Raven. (Why is this important?)

Royal Naval Volunteer Reserve during World War 2

More information about Royal Naval Volunteer Reserve

Formed: 1903

Disbanded: 1958

The present Royal Naval Reserve was formed in 1958 merging the original Royal Naval Reserve (RNR) founded under the Naval Reserve Act in 1859 as a reserve of professional seamen... read more here >>

Collection:	The IWGC/CWGC Registers Collection

THE ROYAL NAVAL Volunteer Reserve was originally a reserve of seamen only, but in 1862 this was extended to include recruitment and training of officers. From its creation the RNVR officers wore a unique, distinctive lace consisting of stripes of interwoven chain. The service was called the "Wavy Navy" after the wavy sleeve stripes that RNVR wore to differentiate them from Royal Navy officers.

From 1938 until 1957 the RNVR provided aircrew personnel in the form of their own Air Branch. After the war it was considered that the training required to operate modern equipment was beyond the expected of reservists and the Air branch squadrons were disbanded.

After 100 years of proud service the RNVR as a separate professional naval service ceased to exist. It was commemorated in London 2003 with a parade on Horse Guards at which HRH Prince Charles took the salute.

The present Royal Naval Reserve was formed in 1958 merging the original Royal Naval Reserve (RNR) founded under the Naval Reserve Act in 1859 as a reserve of professional seamen from the merchant service and fishing fleets and the Royal Naval Volunteer Reserve (RNVR), a reserve of civilian volunteers founded later in 1903.

War Medal 1939 - 1945

The War Medal 1939–1945 was a British decoration awarded to all full time service personnel of the Armed Forces wherever their service during the war was rendered. Operational and non-operational service counted provided personnel had completed 28 days service between 3rd September 1939 and the 2nd September 1945. In the Merchant Navy there was the requirement that 28...

3rd September 1939 and 2nd September 1945. The recipient was awarded this star if their service period was terminated by their death or disability due to service. Also the award of a gallantry medal or mention in Despatched also produced the award of this medal, regardless of...

6.

Sidney John Snow - Naval airman

17th November 1920 – 13th August 1940

Sidney was born to George and Emma Snow in 1920. Theirs was a typical, but impoverished, family living in the East End of London. Sidney had two older siblings, George and Lily.

Little is known of Sidney's early life – although we do know he was named after an uncle who himself had perished in the North Sea on HM Submarine E4 on 15th August 1916.

Like his older sister, who went on to become a radical school mistress, Sidney was academically gifted. He won numerous prizes and 'matriculated' from school at age 16 – no mean feat if you grew up in the working-class East End.

Despite being from a poor background, he was clearly an adventurous individual. At some point in the late 1930s, that adventurous spirit took him alone on a cycling trip to France where he became "lost" and was "rescued" by a Cook's travel agent, who took him under her wing and enabled him to return home to England without further incident.

He was also a keen swimmer and, following a trip to Bavaria to represent Hackney Swimming Club, he returned home enthusiastic about the facilities Germany made available to its young people.

On leaving school, Sidney found himself working as a clerk and telephone operator at the Hope Chemical Works in Hackney, where he was described as "bright and promising". His eventual ambition was to work for HM Customs and Excise.

On the outbreak of war, he answered the call for young men with a matriculation certificate to join the Fleet Air Arm. Having completed his initial training, Sidney was posted on 1st April 1940 to HMS Raven (the wartime name of Southampton Airport).

On 13th August 1940, he was part way through his training at HMS Raven when the Luftwaffe launched "Eagle Day". This was the first day of the Luftwaffe offensive to destroy RAF airfields and gain air supremacy over England in preparation for Operation Sea Lion. The Luftwaffe launched 1,485 sorties, but because of confusion and delays, the main attacks were not mounted until the afternoon. Some airfields were attacked, but not the primary fighter bases. Luftwaffe losses were heavy with 39 aircraft lost (mainly Ju-87 Stuka's), while the RAF lost just 15.

It was on that fateful day that Sidney was killed while training as an air gunner in a two-seater Percival Proctor training aircraft (serial no. P6113) which crashed and burnt out near Winchester, an area of heavy enemy activity.

The family were told very little about the incident, other than the aircraft went into a spin before crashing near Worthy Down. Much of Sidney's kit was sold off to raise funds for his mother and the family were left with a few letters and modest personal effects. The loss his brother, George, felt at the death of his younger brother was always close to the surface and his family conversations would often turn to Sid until George's own death in 1983.

All that remains of Sid's personality are a couple of letters sent to his mother and brother just before he died. The flowing handwriting, turn of phrase and casual enquiries of family and friends reflect a young man looking to the future. References to Peggy, presumably his girlfriend, remind us that he was like so many 19-year-olds, simply trying to live his life and be happy. Yet, in a letter dated 5th August 1940, he gives an indication of the tensions felt at the time:

> *Have you heard about the Fleet Air Arm exploits in the Med. I hope I don't go too far. We were called out at half past five the other morning and we took off, just as the sun was rising, with the old iron creaking under the weight of bombs. You see, in case of an invasion they'd send every ancient old kite to bomb 'em. Even though I've not passed out, it'd not matter – no trade unions now.*

His family can't help but wonder what Sidney, the bright young boy from the poor East End of London, thought when he began to fly with PT Eckersley, such a famous and influential pilot. It's such a tragedy that the lives cut short, experiences, loves and children never experienced, reverberate over 80 years later.

His great-great nephew, born in 2015, was given a teddy bear called Sidney on the day he was born and whenever his great-nephew holidays in France, he thinks of Sidney being rescued from France with his bike all those years ago.

He is not forgotten.

7.

Percival Proctor - the airplane

THE PERCIVAL PROCTOR was a British radio trainer and communications aircraft of the Second World War. It was a single-engined, low-wing monoplane with seating for three or four, depending on the model.

The Proctor was developed from the Percival Vega Gull in response to Air Ministry Specification 20/38 for a radio trainer and communications aircraft. To meet the requirement, it had larger rear cabin windows and the fuselage was six inches (150 mm) longer. Modifications were made to the seats to enable the crew to wear parachutes, and there were other changes to enable a military radio and other equipment to be fitted. In early 1939, an order was placed for 247 aircraft to meet operational requirement OR.65. Proctors were unarmed.

The prototype was tested as an emergency bomber during 1940, but that idea was abandoned when the invasion threat receded. Although the first 222 aircraft were built by Percival at Luton, most of the remaining aircraft were built by F. Hills & Sons of Trafford Park near Manchester. They built 812 Proctors of several marques between 1941 and 1945, assembling most of the aircraft at Barton Aerodrome (Peter Eckersley's home aerodrome).

Whilst the very early Proctors (Mks I to III) followed very closely the last incarnation of the Vega Gull, later versions became much heavier and less aerodynamic, with inevitable detrimental effects upon their performance. The later marques of Proctor, whilst looking broadly similar, were in fact a complete redesign of the aircraft and were much enlarged, heavier and even less efficient. Flight performance was poor.

After their service life, the remaining Proctors soldiered on in private hands until the 1960s, when they were all grounded owing to concerns about the degradation of the glued joints in their wooden airframes. Several surviving Proctors have been rebuilt with modern adhesives. Early Proctors still make good light aircraft because they combine the Vega's attributes of long range, speed and load-carrying ability. Notably, all Proctors inherited the Vega Gull's feature of wing-folding.

A pilot, who flew Proctors with 756 Squadron at Worthy Down, states:

These Proctors were originally the Percival Vega Gull, a sort of rich man's toy but a thoroughly practical light aircraft. Equipped for blind flying, landing lights and powered by a six-cylinder 200hp de Havilland Gipsy Queen engine with a constant speed airscrew, they could cruise when new at about 130mph without undue pushing, but old ones flogged to death, left out in all weather literally for years, became very tired and slow. Nevertheless, they stuck it bravely until condemned by their glued joints opening and fungoid growths sprouting amidst the sodden flooring. They performed a yeoman service in training organisations such as ours. True, wings and tails fell off at times with fatal results, but these happenings were rare.

It is possible that Peter's aircraft had a partial wing failure causing a sudden spin, which could have given little time to react.

8.

Bentley - RA4578

by Martin Crocker

PETER THORP ECKERSLEY was the owner of RA 4578 from 1929 until 1932. Bentley Motors delivered the chassis to the coachbuilders Flewitt & Co of Birmingham in 1927. The company built and fitted the vehicle with a Weymann Saloon body ready for delivery to Gaffikin Wilkinson and Co, Hanover Square, London.

RA4578 at a members track day at the Goodwood Motor Circuit.

The first owner was Kenneth Dobson, a Royal Navy officer from Derbyshire. Kenneth was educated at Repton College and Trinity College, Cambridge and he played cricket for both Derbyshire and Warwickshire County Cricket Clubs and was a goalkeeper for Derby County Football Club. Peter purchased RA 4578 in 1929 when he was living at the Lime House in Lowton, Lancashire.

In 1932 RA4578 was sold to barrister Mr Fox-Andrews before going into the ownership of the MacFarlane family from New Zealand. Laurence Herbert MacFarlane and Francis Maurice MacFarlane were two of four brothers who were all killed during the Second World War. Laurence was shot down over Keil, Germany whilst attacking the Scharnhorst battleship and Francis was killed in a flying training mission near Christchurch, New Zealand.

RA4578 was shipped by Laurence to New Zealand in 1939 and remained there until 2016 when it came into the possession of the current owner, a Mr Lazarus. The Bentley transferred through several owners in New Zealand including the family of Sybil Lupp, the first lady of New Zealand motor racing.

Sybil Lupp servicing RA4578 in 1940.

RA 4578 was actively used in rally events in New Zealand. The photograph below was taken during a hill climb rally in 1948!

During 2016 RA4578 was restored by William Medcalf Ltd at Liss, West Sussex.

Acknowledgements

A big thank you to:

William Eckersley for allowing me access to the family albums and photos of the Eckersley family.

Stephen Chalke has been a great source of encouragement and help with the project, also for writing the forward.

Ken Grime and Andrew Searle for help with the production of the book and the layout and design.

Chris O'Brien for help with Genealogical research.

Keith Pratt for his contacts with World War 2 aircraft research.

Tony Dowland, Alix Hickman and Richard Hall for help with research on Worthy Down and World War 2.

Mark Thomas for help with information about Sydney Smith.

Martin Crocker for help with research about the Bentley which Peter owned.

Rugby School for help with research.

Jeremy Lonsdale for help with the tour to India.

Lancashire CCC library for research.